BASIC
READING POWER

Pleasure Reading • Comprehension Skills
Vocabulary Building • Thinking Skills

SECOND EDITION

Beatrice S. Mikulecky
Linda Jeffries

Longman

longman.com

Pearson Education, 10 Bank Street, White Plains, NY 10606

Executive editor: Laura Le Dréan
Development editor: Dena Daniel
Vice president, director of design and production: Rhea Banker
Executive managing editor: Linda Moser
Production manager: Ray Keating
Production editor: Michael Mone
Director of manufacturing: Patrice Fraccio
Senior manufacturing buyer: Nancy Flaggman
Marketing manager: Joe Chapple
Photo research: Dana Klinek
Cover design: Ann France
Text design: Wendy Wolf
Text composition: Carlisle Communications, Ltd.

Library of Congress Cataloging-in-Publication Data

Mikulecky, Beatrice S.
  Basic reading power : pleasure reading, comprehension skills,
vocabulary building, thinking skills / by Beatrice S. Mikulecky
and Linda Jeffries. — 2nd ed.
      p. cm.
    ISBN 0-13-130549-2 (pbk. : alk. paper)
  1. English language—Textbooks for foreign speakers. 2. Reading
comprehension—Problems, exercises, etc. 3. Thought and
thinking—Problems, exercises, etc. 4. Vocabulary—Problems, exercises,
etc. I. Jeffries, Linda. II. Title.
PE1128.M55 2004
428.614—dc22

                                        2003026796

ISBN: 0-13-130549-2

LONGMAN ON THE **WEB**
Longman.com offers online resources
for teachers and students. Access our
Companion Websites, our online catalog,
and our local offices around the world.

Visit us at **longman.com**.

Printed in the United States of America
1 2 3 4 5 6 7 8 9 10—VHG—08 07 06 05 04

Contents

Acknowledgments

We thank teachers and students for their feedback regarding *Basic Reading Power*. We are especially grateful to the teachers in Japan for their suggestions. We have made every effort to respond to their concerns in this second edition.

About the Authors

Bea Mikulecky holds a master's degree in TESOL and a doctorate in Applied Psycholinguistics from Boston University. In addition to teaching reading, writing, and ESL, she has worked as a teacher-trainer in the Harvard University Summer ESL Program, in the Simmons College MATESL Program, and in Moscow, Russia. Bea Mikulecky is the author of *A Short Course in Teaching Reading Skills* and co-author of the Reading Power series.

Linda Jeffries holds a master's degree in TESOL from Boston University. She has taught reading, writing, and ESL/EFL at Boston College, Boston University, in the Harvard University Summer ESL Program, and at the University of Opole, in Poland. She currently resides in Italy, where she has taught EFL and academic writing at the University of Bologna and the University of Modena. Linda Jeffries is co-author of the Reading Power series.

References

Birch, B.M. *English L2 Reading: Getting to the Bottom,* Lawrence Earlbaum Associates, Publishers, 2002

Carter, R. and M. McCarthy. *Vocabulary and Language Teaching.* Longman, 1988

Day R., ed. *New Ways in Teaching Reading,* TESOL, 1993

Day, R. and J. Bamford. *Extensive Reading in the Second Language Classroom,* Cambridge University Press, 1998

Mikulecky, B. *A Short Course in Teaching Reading Skills,* Addison Wesley Longman, 1990

Introduction

To the Teacher

Basic Reading Power is unlike most other reading textbooks.

- First, the focus is different. This book directs the students' attention to the reading process, while most other books focus primarily on content.
- Second, *Basic Reading Power* is organized to be used in a unique way. The book has *four separate parts* that correspond to four important aspects of proficient reading. It is like four books in one. *Teachers should use and assign work in all four parts of the book concurrently.*

In this, the second edition of *Basic Reading Power,* the approach remains the same. New features have been added and original exercises updated and expanded in response to feedback from teachers. Changes in this new edition:

- Part 1: Pleasure Reading—more emphasis on developing individual vocabulary lists
- Part 2: Comprehension Skills—additional exercises on all the skills
- Part 3: Vocabulary Building—additional exercises and a new unit on Noticing Word Parts
- Part 4: Thinking Skills—additional exercises
- Teacher's Guide—sample syllabus included
- more user-friendly format
- separate Answer Key (not at the back of the student text)

Basic Reading Power is intended for students who are in a beginning-level English program. We assume that the students who use this book will be literate and have an English vocabulary of about 300 words. They should be familiar with the simple present, present continuous, simple past, and future tenses.

The aim of this book is to teach strategies that will allow students to build on their already-established cognitive abilities and background knowledge. A strategic approach will enable students to view reading in English as a problem-solving activity rather than a translation exercise. This way, students can learn good reading habits and skills, and they can avoid problems that commonly result from poor reading habits. Students will gain confidence at this early stage, which, in turn, helps them to gain access more quickly to English-language material for study, work, or pleasure.

In *Basic Reading Power,* students are expected to *work on all four parts of the book concurrently* as they develop multiple aspects of their reading ability. This approach is essential for the successful outcome of a reading program using this book. *Basic Reading Power* is intended to prepare students for work in *Reading Power,* which has a similar general approach and layout.

The Teacher's Guide presents details on using all of the exercises in this book as well as a sample syllabus (pages 183–198).

A note about the Answer Key: In this second edition of *Basic Reading Power,* the Answer Key is supplied as a separate booklet. It is <u>not</u> included at the back of the student text.

To the Student

Basic Reading Power can help you read well in English. In this book, you can work on reading in four ways:

1. Pleasure Reading—read many stories and books
2. Comprehension Skills—understand what you read
3. Vocabulary Building—learn many new words
4. Thinking Skills—learn to think in English

Work on all four parts of the book every week. You can learn to be a good reader in English!

Questionnaire

Answer the questions. Then talk to other students about your answers.

1. What is your name? _____

2. Where do you live? _____

3. What country do you come from? _____

4. What is your first language? _____

5. Do you like to read? _____

6. Do your parents or friends like to read? _____

7. What do you read in your language?

   ☐ books   ☐ magazines

   ☐ newspapers   ☐ other

8. What do you read in English? _____

9. How many books do you read in one year? _____

10. Do you have a favorite book or writer? Write the title or name: _____

   _____

Vocabulary in *Basic Reading Power*

This exercise gives you some new words. These words are in the exercises in this book. Read the sentences. Can you do what they say?

1. Draw a circle around the last word in this sentence.

2. There is a picture of a house on the next page. Draw a circle around the house.

3. A word is missing from this _____. Write in the word.

4. There are two blanks in the next sentence. Think of some words. Write them in the blanks.

5. My _____ goes to _____ every day.

6. Draw a line from number 6 to number 1.

7. One word in this snetnece is not correct. Write that word correctly in the blank. _____

8. Cross out the first word in this sentence. Then cross out the last word in this sentence.

9. Underline the second word in this sentence.

10. Draw a garden near the house on the next page. Follow the steps in number 11.

11. Step 1. Draw a tree.

    Step 2. Draw some flowers.

    Step 3. Draw some grass.

12. Talk about your garden with another student. Are your gardens the same or different?

Which words were new for you? Write them here.

_____

_____

_____

_____

_____

PART 1

Pleasure Reading

Good readers read a lot of stories and books. They read for pleasure, not only for school or work. This part of the book is for pleasure reading. You are going to read and talk about many stories. You can learn to be a good reader in English.

Understanding a Story with New Vocabulary

Sometimes stories have words you don't know. Do you need to know all the words? No! You can understand the story without some words.

Read these paragraphs. Many words are not there. Answer the questions after the paragraphs.

1. Magda is a student at Poznan University in Poland. She's 23 years old. She xxxxx in Mosina. It's a small xxxx near Poznan. Every day, Magda takes xxx train to the city. She goes xx her classes at the university. After her xxxxxxx, she studies with her friends. Sometimes, xxxx have dinner at a restaurant. Xxxx she takes the train home. She xxxxxxx all evening. She wants to be x doctor. She must study hard for xxxx years!

   a. Does Magda live in Poznan? _____

   b. Does she take the train to Poznan? _____

   c. Does she always go home for dinner? _____

   d. What is she studying? _____

2. Gerald is a student at Harvard University in Cambridge, Massachusetts. He's 20 years old. Xx is from a small xxxx in California. He can't xx home very often. Gerald xx studying Chinese. He wants xx go to China next xxxx. In China, he can learn Xxxxxxx well. He can also xxxxx about the country. Some xxx, Gerald wants to work xx business. He wants to xxx and sell things in Xxxxx. But first he must xxxxx how to speak Chinese.

   a. Where is Gerald from? _____

   b. Does he go home every weekend? _____

   c. Can he speak Chinese? _____

   d. Does he want to teach Chinese? _____

Talk about your answers with another student. Are they the same?

Remember

You do not need to know all the words. When you are reading, don't stop at a new word. Don't look in a dictionary or ask the teacher. Read some more. Sometimes you can guess the word from the context (the other sentences). Sometimes you don't need to know the word. You can understand the story without it.

Reading to Understand Stories

Good readers think and ask questions when they read. Follow these steps as you read the stories in Part 1 of this book.

Step 1. Think before you read.

- Look at the picture if there is one.
- Read the title of the story.
- Can you answer any of these questions?
    - What is the story about?
    - Who is in the story?
    - Where are they?

Step 2. Read the story.

- Don't stop to look up new words in a dictionary.
- Don't ask the teacher or other students about new words.
- Read the story all the way to the end.

Step 3. Talk about the story.

- Talk with another student about these questions:
    - What is the story about?
    - Who is in the story?
    - Where are they?
    - Do you like the story? Why?

Step 4. Learn new words.

- Now read the story again and look for new words. Check the meaning of the words in a dictionary.
- Write the new words on the lines under the story.
- Make a vocabulary list. (See pages 122–124.)

UNIT **1** Fables

The stories in this unit are fables. Fables are short stories about people or animals. They are not true stories, but they give a lesson about life. Every country has its fables.

Fable 1

Step 1. **Think before you read.**

Step 2. **Read the story.**

The Farm Girl and the Milk

Once there was a girl who lived on a farm. Every day she took care of the cows. She milked them, and then she made butter and cheese. One morning, her father said, "You are a good girl. You work very hard. You can have this milk. You can take it to town and sell it. Then you can keep the money and buy something nice."

5 So the farm girl went to town with the milk. On the way, she thought, "This is good milk. I can sell it for a good price. Then I can buy some eggs. I'll keep the eggs and soon I'll have chickens. Chickens grow fast. In a few months, I'll have more eggs and more chickens. Then I can sell the chickens and buy a new dress. It will be a beautiful dress. All the young men will look at me. But I won't talk to

10 them. I'll wait for a rich man or a prince. Yes, I'll marry a prince."

The farm girl was very happy. She walked down the road and closed her eyes. She was thinking about the prince. She didn't look down at the road, so she didn't see a large stone. Her foot hit the stone and down she went. Down went the milk, too, all over the road. And that was the end of the eggs and the chickens, the dress, and the prince.

Step 3. **Talk about the story. What is the lesson?**

Step 4. **Read the story again. Write new words here.**

_____

_____

Fable 2

Step 1. **Think before you read.**

Step 2. **Read the story.**

The Crow Who Wanted to Be a Peacock

Once there was a crow. He liked to fly to far places. One day he flew over the king's garden. The garden was a beautiful place. There were flowers and trees and little lakes. And in the garden there were many peacocks.

Peacocks are very beautiful birds. They have long blue and green feathers. The
5 king loved to look at them. Crows are not beautiful birds. They have short, black feathers. The king never looked at them.

"I want to be a peacock," the crow said. He flew down into the garden. There were some beautiful blue and green peacock feathers on the ground. The crow took the feathers. He put them on top of his short, black feathers. Then he walked
10 around the garden with the peacocks.

For a short time, he lived with the peacocks. But they soon saw he wasn't a peacock. They were very angry. They hit him and said, "Go away! You aren't a peacock!"

The crow went home. But he still had his peacock feathers. He wanted the
15 other crows to see him. He wanted to be the most beautiful crow.

The other crows didn't like this. "Who do you think you are?" they said. "You're just a crow, like us!"

They hit him and took away his peacock feathers. "Go away!" they said. "We don't want you!"
20 So the crow went away. He couldn't live in the king's garden. He wasn't beautiful like a peacock. And now he had no friends.

Step 3. Talk about the story. What is the lesson?

Step 4. Read the story again. Write new words here.

_____

_____

Fable 3

Step 1. Think before you read.

Step 2. Read the story.

The Big Family in the Little House

Once there was a man named Vladimir. He had a big family and he lived in a small house. He wasn't very happy.

One day he went to town. He talked to a wise woman. "Please help me," he said. "My wife and I have six children. We live in a very small house. Eight people
5 in a few rooms! We can't live this way!"

The wise woman listened. She closed her eyes for a minute. Then she asked, "How many animals do you have?"

"We have eight animals. We have a horse, a cow, two pigs, and four chickens," said Vladimir.

10 "Good. Go home now," said the wise woman. "Take all your animals into the house with you."

"In the house!" said Vladimir. But he went home and did what the wise woman told him. The next week, he went back to the wise woman.

"This is terrible!" he said. "The animals eat our food. They fill all the rooms.
15 They sleep in our beds."

The wise woman closed her eyes again. Then she told Vladimir, "Now go home. Take the animals out of the house."

Vladimir went home and took the animals out of the house.

The next day, he went back to the wise woman. This time he was happy.
20 "Thank you, thank you," he said. "It's very different without the animals. Now we can eat and sleep. Now we like our house. Thank you for your help. You are a very wise woman!"

Step 3. Talk about the story. What is the lesson?

Step 4. Read the story again. Write new words here.

_____

_____

Fable 4

Step 1. Think before you read.

Step 2. Read the story.

That's Not the Way to Do It!

Once there was a farmer named Hans. He wanted to sell his horse in town. One morning he started down the road with his young son and the horse. He and his son walked with the horse. They passed some boys.

"That's not the way to do it!" said a boy. "Why is that man walking? He has a
5 horse!"

"He's right," said Hans. He got on the horse and his son walked behind him. Then they saw some women.

"Look at that man!" said a woman. "He's on the horse and his poor boy is walking."

10 "She's right," said Hans. He got down and put his son on the horse. They walked some more.

"Isn't that terrible!" said an old man. "Young people have no love for their parents these days! Look at that boy on the horse. His poor father is walking."

"He's right," says Hans. He got on the horse behind his son. Then they saw
15 some girls.

"Two people on a horse!" said the girls. "The poor animal."

"They're right," said Hans. He and his son got off the horse. They put the horse on their backs and carried it down the road.

They came to a river with a bridge. Some people were fishing from the bridge.
20 "Look at that!" they said. "Look at the horse!" They laughed and laughed.

The horse didn't like this. He moved and kicked. "Help, help," cried Hans. And they all fell off the bridge and into the river—Hans, his son, and the horse.

The horse ran home. Hans and his son climbed out of the river.

"Next time," said Hans, "I'm not going to listen to other people. I'm going to
25 do it my way."

Step 3. Talk about the story. What is the lesson?

Step 4. Read the story again. Write new words here.

_____

_____

Fable 5

Step 1. Think before you read.

Step 2. Read the story.

The Wolf and the Dog

One evening, a wolf was looking for food. He was very hungry. He saw some chickens in a farmyard. He wanted to eat the chickens, but there was a dog in the yard, too. The dog was big and strong. The wolf didn't want to fight the dog, but he was very, very hungry. He waited near the yard.

5   The wolf saw a man come out of the house. The man gave some food to the dog and then went back into the house.

"Good evening," the wolf called to the dog.

"Good evening," said the dog with his mouth full.

The wolf said, "Do you get food every day?"

10   "Two times a day," said the dog. "I get breakfast in the morning and dinner in the evening." He ate some more. Then he looked at the wolf. "Are you hungry? Come live here with me. This is a good life. I help the man and he gives me food."

The dog ate all his dinner and sat down. He said to the wolf, "You are always running and fighting. Your life is not easy. Come live here. Life is easy here."

15   The wolf sat down near the dog. He thought, "Why not? I can eat every day here, and I can have a friend."

But then he looked at the dog.

"What is that under your ears?" he asked.

"What?" said the dog.

20   "Look at your neck! It's all red!" said the wolf.

"Oh, that's nothing," said the dog.

"Nothing!" said the wolf. "It's terrible!"

"No, no," said the dog. "It's because of the chain. During the day, the farmer puts a chain on my neck."

25   "A chain!" said the wolf. "You have to stay there all day? You can't run or hunt?"

"That's right," said the dog. "But I don't care. I sleep all day. And at night I can run around the farmyard."

"Then no thank you, my friend. I can't stay here with you. I don't want a

30 chain on my neck. Goodbye!"

And the wolf ran away, still hungry.

Step 3. Talk about the story. What is the lesson?

Step 4. Read the story again. Write new words here.

_____

_____

Fable 6

Step 1. Think before you read.

Step 2. Read the story.

A Bell on the Cat

Once there was a large family of mice. They lived in a store. There was always food in the store and they were happy. Then more mice came to live there. Soon there were lots and lots of mice in the store.

The storekeeper was not happy about this. One day he went out and got a big,
5   black cat. It was hungry and it liked mice.

The mice didn't know what to do. "This cat is terrible," said a mother mouse. "It'll catch my children and eat them!"

"We must talk to our president. He always knows what to do," said another mouse.

10   They went to the president. "Mr. President," they said, "we are afraid of this cat. It is going to kill us all if we don't do something. But what can we do?"

The president was a big, old mouse. He said, "We must have a meeting. All the mice must come."

And so there was a meeting of all the mice. The president of the mice came in
15   and stood up.

"My dear friends," he said, "we are living in a bad time. A big, black cat is here in our store. This terrible animal wants to catch us and eat us. But, my friends, I know what to do. Your president always has the answer. We can put a bell on the cat. That way we can hear it coming. And we can run away in time."

20   "Hurrah!" said all the mice. "Our president is very wise." The mice were all happy. "Isn't he a wise mouse?" they said. "Isn't he a good president?"

    But then a young mouse said, "Mr. President, I have a question."

    "Yes," said the president.

    "Please," said the young mouse, "who is going to put the bell on the cat?"

25   "Not I! Not I!" said all the mice. Then they stopped talking. They looked at the president. He said nothing. All the mice ran out of the meeting. And the next day, they moved out of the store.

Step 3. Talk about the story. What is the lesson?

Step 4. Read the story again. Write new words here.

_____

_____

Fable 7

Step 1. Think before you read.

Step 2. Read the story.

The Boy and the Wolf

Once a boy named Kamal lived in a little village. Every day he went out with his father's sheep. He stayed with the sheep all day. In the evening he came back to the village.

One day, the boy thought, "I don't like this! I'm with the sheep all day. The
5 sheep don't talk, and they don't listen to me. There's nothing to do!"

Kamal sat there for some time. Then he said, "I know!" He jumped up and began to shout, "Wolf! Wolf!"

In a few minutes, people came running from the village.

"Where is the wolf?" they asked.

10 "Oh, there's no wolf," said the boy. "I wanted to see you and talk to you."

The people were not happy. They went back to the village. "That bad boy!" they said.

The next day, Kamal was out with his sheep. Again, he didn't want to be alone, so he shouted, "Wolf! Wolf!"

15 Again, the people came running from the village. This time, they were very angry. "Don't do that again!" they said. "Next time, we won't come. We have work to do. We can't come here to talk with you!" And they went back to their work.

That same afternoon, Kamal was alone with the sheep again. He was almost asleep. Then he heard something behind the trees. He opened his eyes. It was a wolf. The wolf was coming to eat the sheep. "Help! Help!" shouted Kamal. "There's a wolf!"

The people in the village heard the boy, but this time they didn't come. So Kamal ran away and the wolf killed the sheep.

20

Step 3. Talk about the story. What is the lesson?

Step 4. Read the story again. Write new words here.

_____

_____

Fable 8

Step 1. Think before you read.

Step 2. Read the story.

The Bear and the Two Friends

One day, two friends were out for a walk.
"What a beautiful day!" said Alik.
"Yes, this is a good day for a walk," said Stefan. "It's not raining, and it's not hot."

So they talked and walked for a long time. The road went around a mountain
5   and through lots of trees. Suddenly, Alik stopped talking. He ran to a tree and
climbed up. Then he called down to Stefan. "Run, Stefan. There's a bear!"

Stefan didn't have time to run. He didn't have time to climb a tree. So he fell to
the ground and didn't move.

The bear walked over to him and looked at him. He made noises in Stefan's ear.
10 Stefan still didn't move. After some time, the bear went away. Bears don't eat dead
people or animals.

Then Alik came down from the tree.

"Sorry," he said. "I wanted to tell you about the bear. But I didn't have time."

Stefan said nothing. He got up from the ground.
15 "What did the bear say to you?" asked Alik.

"He told me something very important," said Stefan.

"What was that?" asked Alik.

"He told me that good friends don't run away. They stay to help their friends."
Stefan turned away and walked down the road alone.

Step 3. Talk about the story. What is the lesson?

Step 4. Read the story again. Write new words here.

_____

_____

Fable 9

Sinbad and the Genie

One day, Sinbad the Sailor was by the sea. He sat down by the water. Somebody called to him. There was an old bottle near him. He looked at the bottle. In it, there was a very, very small person. It was a genie.

"Help! Help!" said the genie. "Please let me out."

5   Sinbad opened the bottle. A big, gray cloud came out. In the cloud, there was a very, very big genie.

"Thank you, sailor. And now, I'm going to eat you. My last meal was 5,000 years ago. I'm very hungry."

The genie was very big and strong, and he had Sinbad in his hand. Sinbad was 10 small and not very strong. But he was clever.

He said to the genie, "How can you eat me—a little thing like you?"

"Little?" said the genie, in a terrible way. "I'm very big!"

"How can you be very big?" asked Sinbad. "You were in this little bottle!"

"I changed," said the genie. "Can't you see how big I am now?"

15   "No, no," said Sinbad. "I see only a little bottle."

The genie's face was all red. He was very terrible to see. "I'll show you!" he said. "Look at me! I'll change again."

The genie went into his big, gray cloud. Then the cloud went away. The genie was little, and he was inside the bottle again.

20   Sinbad was clever and he was also fast. The top was on the bottle again and the genie couldn't come out. Sinbad put the bottle in the sea and walked away.

"Goodbye for another 5,000 years!" he said.

Step 3. Talk about the story. What is the lesson?

Step 4. Read the story again. Write new words here.

_____

_____

Fable 10

Step 1. **Think before you read.**

Step 2. **Read the story.**

The Strongest Person

Once there was a girl mouse named Mariko and a boy mouse named Nazumi. They were in love and they wanted to get married. But Mariko's parents said no. Mariko could only marry the strongest person in the world. "Who's the strongest person in the world?" they asked.

5   They looked up at the sky. "The sun is the strongest person," they said. They asked the sun, "Do you want to marry our daughter?"

"Your daughter is very beautiful," said the sun. "But I'm not the strongest person. The cloud is stronger. He can stop my light."

So Mariko's parents called to the cloud. "Are you the strongest person?" they
10 asked.

The cloud answered, "No, no. I'm not the strongest person. The wind is stronger. I must go where he tells me."

"Oh, wind," said Mariko's parents. "What do you say? Are you very strong?"

"Yes, yes," said the wind. "I'm very strong. But a high wall can stop me."

15   The mice parents talked to a high wall. "Please, wall, can you answer our question? We're looking for the strongest person in the world. Are you that person?"

The wall said, "I'm very strong. But look at my feet. There are many holes in the ground below me. Nazumi, the mouse, made those holes."

20   Mariko's parents looked at the holes. Then they went to look for Nazumi. "Nazumi," they said, "you are the strongest person in the world. Do you want to marry our daughter?"

"Yes!" said Nazumi. And so Mariko married Nazumi, and they were very happy.

Step 3. **Talk about the story. What is the lesson?**

Step 4. **Read the story again. Write new words here.**

_____

_____

Fable 11

Step 1. Think before you read.

Step 2. Read the story.

The Turtle and the Ducks

Once there was a turtle. He was not very happy. "Here I am on the ground," he said. "I can't go fast. I can't see things far away. I can only see the ground and the grass. Poor, poor me."

Then the turtle looked up at the sky. "Look at those birds," he said. "They go to
5 faraway places. They see many things. I want to be a bird. I want to fly, too."

Two ducks stopped near the turtle.

"Oh, ducks," asked the turtle. "What can I do? I want to go to far places. I want to see the world."

"I think we can help you," said the ducks.
10   "Can you?" asked the turtle. "How?"

"You can fly with us to Africa or to America. You can see mountains, oceans, and cities—all the things you want to see."

"But how can I fly?" asked the turtle.

"With a stick," said the ducks. "We can hold a stick in our mouths. You can
15 hold on to it with your mouth. Then we can carry you through the air."

And that's what they did. The ducks went up in the air with the turtle. They flew for a long time. The turtle saw many new things. He saw rivers and mountains and the sea. He saw a city and lots of people.

The people also saw the turtle. "A turtle in the air!" they said. "Run, run to the
20 queen. There's a flying turtle. She must see it."

The queen came out of her castle. "Where is the turtle?" she asked.

"Here! Can't you see me?" shouted the turtle. But when he spoke, he opened his mouth. And when he opened his mouth, he fell to the ground and died.

Step 3. Talk about the story. What is the lesson?

Step 4. Read the story again. Write new words here.

_____

_____

Fable 12

Step 1. Think before you read.

Step 2. Read the story.

The Fisherman and His Wife

Once there was a fisherman. He and his wife lived in a little house by the sea. They were very poor.

One day the fisherman went out in his boat. He wanted to catch some fish for dinner. For many hours, he caught nothing. Then, in the evening, he caught a big,
5 fat fish.

"Please don't eat me!" said the fish. "I'm not like other fish. Tell me what you want. I can give it to you."

The fisherman put the fish back into the sea. He went home and told his wife about the fish. She said, "Husband! I don't like this old house. Tell the fish I want a
10 new house."

So the fisherman went back to the sea. He called to the fish, "Oh, fish! My wife wants a new house!"

"Go home," said the fish. "Your wife has a new house."

The fisherman went home. His wife was in a nice, new house. There were
15 flowers in the yard, and she was very happy.

But the next morning, she wasn't happy. She said to her husband, "This house is very small. I want a big house now. Go back to the fish and tell him."

So the fisherman went back to the sea. "Oh, fish!" he called. "My wife wants a big house now."

20 "Go home," said the fish. "Your wife has a big house."

The fisherman went home. There was his wife in a very big and beautiful house. She was very happy.

But the next morning she said, "A big house is nice. But it's not enough. I want to be a queen!"

25 So the fisherman went back to the sea again. "Oh, fish!" he called. "My wife wants to be a queen now."

"Go home," said the fish. "Your wife is a queen."

The fisherman went home. His wife was now a queen. She had on a beautiful dress. "Now you can be happy," said the fisherman to his wife.

30 The next morning it rained. The fisherman's wife said, "I don't like the rain. Tell the fish I want to stop the rain."

So the fisherman went back to the sea another time. "Oh, fish!" he called. "Help me! My wife is still not happy. She wants to stop the rain."

"Go home," said the fish. "Your wife asks for too much! Now she has nothing."

35 The fisherman went home. His wife was in their old house again. And once again, they were very poor.

Step 3. Talk about the story. What is the lesson?

Step 4. Read the story again. Write new words here.

_____

_____

UNIT 2   Stories

The stories in this unit are not fables. They are about people and places in different countries. Some stories are about the present and some are about the past.

Remember the Four Reading Steps

- Think before you read.
- Read the story.
- Talk about the story.
- Read the story again. Learn new words.

Story 1

The Man with the Gloves

Michael Greenberg lived in New York. Every day he walked to work. He walked fast, like the other people in New York. He looked down at the ground. He didn't look at the people in the street.

One winter day, Michael was late for work. He walked very fast around a
5   corner. He ran into an old man and the man fell down. Michael stopped to help him. The old man didn't have warm clothes. Michael saw his hands. They were blue with cold!

Michael took off his gloves and gave them to the old man. The old man looked at the gloves and he looked at Michael. Then he put the gloves on his hands.
10   Michael said goodbye. The old man just looked at the gloves and smiled.

That evening, Michael had no gloves. His hands got very cold! He looked at the people on the street, and he saw other people with no gloves. They were poor people. They had no home and they lived on the streets. Michael wanted to help these people. What could he do? He went to a store and bought some
15   gloves.

The next morning, he saw a woman with no gloves. He opened his bag and took out some gloves. The woman said no. She didn't have money for gloves. But Michael put the gloves on her hands. Then he saw another woman with no gloves. She had two children with her. He gave them gloves, too. The gloves were very big,
20   but they were warm.

Michael bought more gloves that evening. He bought big gloves for men and women and little gloves for children. He gave them all away. After that, he always had gloves in his bag. The poor people soon knew Michael well. They called him "Gloves" Greenberg. "Here comes Gloves," they said.
25   And so, for more than 25 years, Michael gave gloves to the poor people in New York. "A pair of gloves is a small thing," he said, "but it can make a big difference to people in the winter in New York."

Write new words here.

_____

_____

A Very Special Party

In 1995, Amalya Antonovna lived in St. Petersburg, Russia. She was 75 years old, and she lived alone. Her husband was dead. Her son, Pavel, was also dead, she thought. She last saw him in 1945. After that, for 50 years she had no news of him.

5   What happened in 1945? That was a time of war in Europe. Pavel's father was a soldier. He was killed in the war in 1942. After that, Amalya was alone with her baby. Those were terrible times in Russia. There was very little food. The winter was very cold. The German army was in Russia. German soldiers killed many Russians. They sent many other Russians to Germany to work. Many of these

10   people got sick and died.

    Amalya was a Russian worker in Germany. At the end of the war, she was still alive. Pavel was still alive, too. But Amalya was very sick. The English and American armies came to the town. Amalya asked some English soldiers for help. "Take my little boy," she said. "I am very sick, but he must live."

15   So Pavel went to England. He went to live with an English family, the Corbetts. He was just three years old. Grace and George Corbett were very good to Pavel. He was a son to them. They gave him an English name—Paul. They never told him about his Russian mother.

    Paul Corbett married and had two children. When he was 45, Grace Corbett

20   died. Then George Corbett told him about his Russian mother. Paul wanted to look for her. Maybe she was dead after all these years. But maybe not.

    He sent many letters to Russia. Several years passed. Then one day a letter came from St. Petersburg. Amalya was alive and well, and she wanted very much to see him. So Paul Corbett went with his family to St. Petersburg.

25   Amalya had a big party. All her friends came to meet her son. There was lots of good Russian food and music. Amalya didn't speak any English. Paul and his family didn't speak any Russian. But words were not important. They were all happy.

Write new words here.

_____

_____

Christmas Gifts

Christmas was a big day for John and Adele. They always had a very nice dinner. Then they opened their presents. Often the presents were small things. John and Adele did not have much money. But John always had something for Adele, and Adele always had something for John.

5   It was the day before Christmas. But this year John and Adele still did not have any presents. They didn't have any money for presents. "We're happy without them," they said.

But it wasn't true. John wanted to buy something for his wife. And Adele wanted to buy something for her husband.

10 Adele went into town. She looked at the store windows. There were many beautiful things in the windows. In the window of a music store, she saw some CDs. There was a new CD by Pavarotti. John loved music, and he loved Pavarotti. Adele wanted to buy that CD for John, but she didn't have the money.

Then she remembered her hair. Adele had very long, beautiful red hair. Her
15 hairdresser wanted to cut it and buy it from her. Adele always said no. But now she went to the hairdresser and said yes.

She went back to the music store with the money, and she bought the Pavarotti CD.

When Adele came home, John was already there.
20 "What do you think?" Adele asked him. "Do you like my new Christmas haircut?"

"Oh, no!" John said.

"You don't like it?" Adele said.

"Why did you do that?" John asked.

"I wanted to buy something for you," said Adele. "So I sold my hair. Here is
25 your present."

John opened the present. "Oh, Adele!" he said. "This is terrible!"

"You mean you don't like the CD?" asked Adele.

"No, no. Thank you. It's wonderful," said John. "But I don't have a CD player now. I needed money for your present, and my friend George needed a CD player.
30 So I sold the CD player to him. Here's your present."

Adele opened a small box. In it there were two combs for her hair. They were very beautiful, but now her hair was very short. She couldn't use combs!

"I can use them next year," she said. "Thank you, my love."

"And someday soon I'm going to get another CD player," John said. He smiled.
35 "You know, Adele, you're beautiful with short hair!"

Write new words here.

_____

_____

_____

The Telephone Call

Camille was three years old. She lived in a small town in France. Her father worked far away in the city. Her mother worked in the house.

One Saturday, Camille's mother fell down on the floor. Her eyes were closed. She didn't move. Camille's father was home. He called the doctor on the

5 telephone. The doctor came to help Camille's mother. In a few days, she was well.

Then one day she fell down again. This time, Camille's father was not home. There was only Camille. She looked at her mother on the floor, and she was afraid. She started to cry. Then she remembered the telephone. She went to the telephone. She did the same thing her father did. She pushed some numbers on

10 the telephone.

A man answered her call. He was Claude Armand, an engineer. His office was in the city. He didn't know Camille. At first, he didn't understand her.

Camille said, "Mommy, Mommy!"

"Where's your mother?" asked Claude Armand.

15 "She's lying down," said Camille. "She can't get up." Camille started to cry.

Claude Armand wanted to help Camille. "Where do you live?" he asked.

"Near my grandma," she answered. She didn't know her street or her town. She was only three!

Then Claude Armand said to her, "Don't put down the telephone. Talk to me

20 some more. Tell me about your daddy. Where is he?"

He asked her lots of questions. At the same time, a friend in his office called the telephone company. She told the telephone company about Camille's mother. She said they needed Camille's address. The telephone company told the police. The police told the government in Paris. Then the government said okay to the

25 police. The police said okay to the telephone company. And the telephone company told them Camille's address.

All this time, Camille talked with Claude Armand. She told him about her house and her family. She told him about her grandparents, her friends, and her little cat. They talked for 45 minutes!

30 Then the police were at Camille's house with a doctor. They called to her and rang the doorbell. Camille said goodbye to Claude Armand and went to open the door. Now she was not alone anymore. Now her mother was okay.

Write new words here.

_____

_____

Story 5

What's in the Back Seat?

Laura Simon lived in Chicago. One winter day, she saw that she had no more milk in her refrigerator. She put her baby in the car, and she drove to the store. It was only ten minutes away. But in five minutes, the baby was asleep.

Laura stopped in front of the store. She looked at the sleeping baby. She didn't
5   want to wake him up. There was a coat on the back seat. She put it over the baby and went into the store. The car key was still in the car.

At that moment, Todd Jenkins walked by. He was cold, and he didn't have a warm place to go. He saw the key in Laura Simon's car and decided to take the car. He got in and drove away.

10   After five minutes, there was a noise in the car. What was that? Todd drove some more. Then he stopped. There was something in the car. He looked at the back seat and saw a coat. The noise came from under the coat. He moved the coat, and there was a baby!

Todd looked at the baby. The baby looked at him and smiled. "Daa Daa," said
15   the baby.

"No, I'm not your daddy," said Todd. He got out of the car and walked away. Then he looked back. The baby started to cry. Todd went back to the car. The baby stopped crying and smiled again. "Daa Daa," he said.

Todd got back in the car and drove some more. The baby was happy. But after a
20   few minutes, he started to cry. "Waa waa," he said.

"What do you want?" asked Todd.

"Waa waa," cried the baby.

"Are you hungry?" asked Todd. "I don't have any milk. Now what can I do? He's hungry!"

25   Todd looked at the baby. The baby looked at Todd.

"Waa waa!" cried the baby again.

"Okay, okay," Todd said. He drove back to the store. Laura Simon was there. A policeman and policewoman were there, too.

Todd Jenkins got out of the car. "I think your baby is hungry," he said to Laura
30   Simon.

"My poor baby!" said Laura Simon, and she ran to the car.

"Never again!" said Todd Jenkins to the police, and they took him away.

Write new words here.

_____

_____

A Day Trip to Mexico

Seattle is a city by the sea. There are lots of boats in Seattle. Some of the boats are fishing boats. Some boats go to faraway places. Some boats go to the San Juan Islands nearby.

Anthony Brewer lived in Seattle. He was 16 years old, and he wanted to go
5 away. It was the end of the school year, and it was hot. Anthony's friends were on the San Juan Islands. He wanted to go there, too.

One morning, Anthony had an idea. He didn't tell his parents about his idea. They were at work. He went down to the boats. He couldn't buy a ticket for the San Juan Islands. He didn't have very much money. He walked by the boats.
10 Which one went to the San Juan Islands? He didn't want to ask because he didn't want people to see him.

Then he saw a sign on a boat. It said San Juan. Anthony looked around. He didn't see any people, so he got on the boat. There were some large boxes on the boat. He got into a box and closed it. After a few minutes, he heard some men on
15 the boat. Soon the boat started to move. Anthony saw the buildings of Seattle, and then he saw only the sea.

It was a warm day. Anthony was happy in the box. The boat moved up and down a little. Soon he was asleep. He slept for two hours. Two hours! Why were they still at sea? The San Juan Islands were only an hour from Seattle. He looked
20 out and saw only the sea all around. He listened to the people on the boat, but he could not understand them. Maybe this wasn't the boat for the San Juan Islands! What boat was it? Where was it going?

Anthony didn't know what to do. He sat in the box all day. Night came and it was very cold in the box. He had no warm clothing, no food, and nothing to
25 drink. Now he wanted to go home!

The next morning, some men opened the box. They saw Anthony, and they pulled him out. Anthony was afraid. But the men smiled, and they gave him some food and water.

"Where is the boat going?" he asked.
30 "To Mexico," they answered.

"Can you stop before that?" he asked. "I have to go home!"

"No," they said. "We can't stop. But we can call your parents on the radio."

Ten days later, Anthony was in Mexico. He went to the Mexican police for help. They put him on a plane to Seattle. His parents came to get him at the
35 airport. The airplane ticket cost them $500, but they weren't angry. They were happy to see Anthony again.

"I wanted to go away," said Anthony, "but not to Mexico! I only wanted to go on a day trip."

Write new words here.

_____

_____

Story 7

Young Love

In 1942, Italy was at war. Antonio was a soldier in the Italian army. He was in a small city in Tunisia. In this city, there was a hotel. The manager of the hotel was also Italian.

Antonio often went to the hotel. He was a friend of the manager and his
5   family. He liked to talk with them about Italy and about the end of the war. The manager's daughter, Sabrina, was 19. She was very beautiful. Antonio liked her very much and wanted to talk with her, but she didn't like to talk to soldiers.

So Antonio watched her and waited. Then, one day, she smiled at him. He smiled at her, and they started talking. They talked and talked. In a short time,
10   they were in love, and they wanted to get married. But her parents said, "You can't get married now because of the war. You must wait."

Soon the war was close to the city. One day, Antonio went to see Sabrina. He was very sad. "I must leave tomorrow with the army," he said. "The British army is going to be here soon."
15   Sabrina cried and cried. Antonio cried, too. He was at the hotel with Sabrina and her family all night. He went away with the first light. Antonio and Sabrina stopped at the door for a last kiss. Then he walked away. At the end of the street, he looked back. Sabrina was still there at the door.

The war didn't go well for the Italian army. The British army took many Italian
20   soldiers with them. Antonio was one of these soldiers. The English sent him to India. He was there for four years.

Antonio sent many letters to Sabrina, but the letters all came back to him. Where was Sabrina? Was she still alive? He didn't get any answers to his questions.

Then, in 1946, Antonio went back to Italy. He went to work in Milan. He got
25   married, and soon he had two children. One day, in 1961, he was in Rome, and he saw Sabrina in a store. He went into the store.

At first, she was happy to see him, but then she cried. They went into a café and had some coffee. Sabrina now lived in Rome. She was married and had three children. She was happy with her life.

30   "But," she said, "I waited for many years. I waited for you. We had to leave Tunisia and I never got your letters."

It was time for Antonio to get his train back to Milan. They went out into the street and said goodbye. Antonio went back to his family in Milan, and Sabrina went back to her family in Rome. Antonio never saw Sabrina again.

Write new words here.

_____

_____

Story 8

Man's Best Friend

Rudy was a large, brown dog. He was from Hamburg, Germany, but he was not at home very often. He was in a truck on the roads of Europe with his friend, Heinrich.

Rudy and Heinrich often lived in the truck for many days. They stopped at
5   restaurants for their meals. They had beds on the truck. On long drives, Heinrich didn't want to fall asleep. So he talked to Rudy and Rudy listened.

In Hamburg, they lived with Heinrich's sister, Elena. At home, Heinrich and Rudy liked to sleep a lot. They also went for long walks, or they went to see Heinrich's friends. Rudy always went with Heinrich.

10   One evening, Rudy and Heinrich didn't come home. In the morning, Elena called Heinrich's friends. They did not know about Heinrich. Then there was a noise at the door. Elena opened the door, and there was Rudy. He was alone. He barked at her and wanted her to go out with him. Elena called the police. After some time, the police called her back. Heinrich was in the hospital. He had a heart
15   problem and he was very sick.

Elena went to the hospital to see her brother. His eyes were closed, and he didn't talk. The doctor said Heinrich was not in danger anymore but was still very sick.

The next day, Heinrich opened his eyes. He asked about Rudy.

Poor Rudy. He was at home, waiting for Heinrich. He waited and waited by the
20   door. He didn't want to get up, and he didn't want to eat. Elena took him to the animal doctor. The doctor looked at Rudy and said, "This dog isn't sick. He's sad."

Elena told Heinrich about Rudy. Heinrich said, "Give Rudy my hat."

Elena went home with the hat. Rudy put his nose to the hat. He moved his tail. He ate some food and got up from the floor. But he didn't move away from
25   the door. The next day he stopped eating again.

Then Elena went to Heinrich's doctor. She told him about Rudy. "Can I bring Rudy to the hospital?" she asked.

"No," said the doctor. "No dogs in the hospital." The doctor was sorry for Rudy. He talked to some other doctors. In the end, they said, "Okay. There's a little
30 room near the hospital door. Rudy can meet Heinrich in that room."

Elena went to the hospital with Rudy. He was very thin, and he walked very slowly. But when he saw Heinrich, he jumped up and barked and barked. Heinrich was on a bed. He smiled and talked to Rudy. And after that, Rudy started to eat again. He started to run and play again.

Write new words here.

_____

_____

Story 9

A Man and Many Wolves

Farley Mowat worked for the Canadian government. The government wanted to know more about wolves. Do wolves kill lots of caribou (big animals)? Do they kill people? The government told Farley to learn about wolves.

They gave him lots of food and clothes and guns. Then they put him on a
5 plane and took him to a place in the far north. There were no houses or people in this place. But there were lots of animals—and lots of wolves.

People tell terrible stories about wolves. They say wolves like to kill and eat people. Farley remembered these stories, and he was afraid. He had his gun with him all the time.
10 Then one day, he saw a group of wolves. There was a mother wolf with four baby wolves. A father wolf and another young wolf lived with them.

Farley watched these wolves every day. The mother was a very good mother. She gave milk to her babies. She gave them lessons about life. They learned how to get food. The father wolf got food for the mother. The young wolf played with the
15 children. They were a nice, happy family—a wolf family!

Farley did not need his gun anymore. In a short time, he and the wolf family were friends. Farley watched them for five months. He learned many new things about wolves. He learned that many stories about wolves weren't true. Wolves don't eat people, and they don't eat many large animals. The large animals they
20 eat are often old or sick.

What do they eat most of the time? Lots of small animals. For example, they eat lots and lots of mice. Can a large animal live on mice? Farley wanted to know. There was only one way to learn. He was a large animal, too—a large man. He

25　must try to live on mice! So he did. He ate mice—and no other food—for two weeks. After that, he didn't want any more mice! But he wasn't thin, and he wasn't sick. Yes, a man can live on mice, so a wolf can, too. Now he could answer the government's questions about wolves.

In that far place, Farley didn't see many people. But he learned bad things
30　about some men. These men told terrible stories about wolves. In the stories, wolves killed hundreds of caribou. But this wasn't true. Farley learned that the men killed the caribou. They also killed many wolves.

Farley Mowat never saw the wolf family again. But he wrote a book about them. The book is called *Never Cry Wolf*. He wanted people to understand wolves
35　and to stop killing them.

Write new words here.

_____

_____

Story 10

Ben and Jerry's

Ben Cohen and Jerry Greenfield both came from Merrick, New York. They were good friends. After college, they wanted to start a business together. What kind of business? A food business, of course. Ben and Jerry were different in many ways, but in one way they were the same. They liked food!
5　One food they liked very much was ice cream. They wanted to open an ice-cream shop. Where was a good place for an ice-cream shop? They looked at many cities and towns. Then they went to Burlington, Vermont. They liked the city a lot. It had lots of young people, and it did not have any good ice-cream shops. There was only one problem with Burlington. For five months of the year, it was very
10　cold there. Did people buy ice cream on cold days?

On May 5, 1978, Ben and Jerry opened their ice-cream shop. It was a small shop, and it wasn't very beautiful. But the ice cream was very good. Lots of people came to eat ice cream on opening day. They came back again and again. There were always lots of people in the shop. Ben and Jerry worked very hard. One
15　night after work, Ben was very tired. He went to sleep on the ground in front of the shop!

After a few months, Ben and Jerry went to the bank. They had bad news. There were only a few dollars in their bank account.

"Why is that?" they asked. "After all these months of hard work!"
20　Then they started to learn about business. They learned about costs and expenses. And they learned about marketing and sales. They started to have big

ice-cream parties. They gave free ice cream on some days. People in other cities learned about Ben and Jerry's, and they came a long way to eat the ice cream.

25 Ben and Jerry made more ice cream, and they started selling it to stores and restaurants. First, they went to stores and restaurants in Vermont. Then they started selling their ice cream to stores across the United States. By 1988, they were selling ice cream all over the United States. A few years later, people could also buy their ice cream in Canada, Great Britain, Russia, and Israel.

Why do people buy Ben and Jerry's ice cream? First of all, it is very, very
30 good ice cream. It is made with good Vermont milk, and it does not have any chemicals in it. People also buy Ben and Jerry's ice cream because they like the company.

From the beginning, Ben and Jerry wanted their company to be different. They didn't just want to make money. They also wanted to help people in many ways.
35 Ben and Jerry's is now a very big company, and Ben and Jerry don't work there any more. But the company still helps people. They give jobs to lots of people. And they give money—7.5% of the money they make—to help children and sick people in the United States and in other countries.

Write new words here.

_____

_____

Story 11

Read a Book—or Go to Jail!

Stan Rosen lived in New Bedford, Massachusetts. He stole cars and bicycles from people. One day, the police caught him and sent him to jail.

The next year, Stan was out of jail. He told some people his name was Jim Rosen. He got money from them for a business. Then he ran away with the
5 money. The police caught him again and sent him to jail.

The year after that, Stan was home again. One night, he stole some money from a store, and again, the police caught him. But this time, they sent him to Judge Kane.

Judge Kane asked Stan, "Do you want to go to jail again? Or do you want to read books?"
10 Stan didn't understand.

"This time," said the judge, "you can decide. You can read books with Professor Waxler at the New Bedford High School. Or you can go to jail."

Stan was 27 years old. He didn't have a high school degree. He didn't read very much. He didn't like reading! But he didn't want to go to jail again. So he decided
15 to read books in Professor Waxler's class. "You must go to every class," said Judge Kane. "And you must read all the books."

Stan went to the first class. There were ten men in the class, and all of the men were sent by Judge Kane. In the first class, they read a short story.

Professor Waxler asked, "What did you think about it?"

20   The men said nothing. They didn't know how to talk about stories. Stan wanted to answer the question, but he was afraid to talk. He didn't want the other men to hear him.

"Did you like the story?" Professor Waxler asked him.

"No," said Stan.

25   "Why not?" asked Professor Waxler.

"Because the end was happy, but life isn't happy," said Stan.

"That's not true," said another man. "Life is happy for some people."

Then other men started talking about the story and about life. They talked for two hours. Professor Waxler told them to read a book for the next class. It was a

30 book about a young man with many problems.

At the next class, Professor Waxler asked again, "What did you think?"

This time the men were not afraid to answer. They had lots of ideas about the book, and they talked a lot about their lives. For 12 weeks, Stan read books and talked about them. Then he had to decide again: Go to class or go to jail. He

35 decided to go to class.

After that, Stan took evening classes at the high school. He went to work in the daytime. The next year, he started evening classes at the university. Now Stan is a good student—and he has no problems with the police. Thanks to Judge Kane and Professor Waxler—and some books.

Write new words here.

_____

_____

Story 12

Who Took the Money?

Manuel lived in a village in Spain called Santa Maria. It was a small village in the mountains. At 15, Manuel started working on the Spanish trains. Every Monday morning, he went by train down to the city. He came back home again on Friday evening. He worked for long hours, and he worked hard.

5   When he was 24, he married Maria. She was from the next village. They had two daughters, Sofia and Lucinda. Manuel didn't see his family very much. He was away for five days a week. But he had a good job, and that was important.

Santa Maria was a poor village. Many men there didn't have good jobs. They worked only a few months every year. Their families did not have money for meat

10 or coffee. Their children did not have good coats or shoes. But Manuel's daughters

always had good coats and shoes. The family had meat, coffee, and many good things to eat. On Sundays, Sofia and Lucinda had ice cream after dinner.

But not all Manuel's money went to his family. Every month, he put a little money in the bank. He didn't tell Maria about this.

15 "A little money in the bank is important," he thought. "But money can be a bad thing. People can get angry and fight about it. I'm not going to tell my wife and daughters about this money. Not now. Someday I'll tell them, and we'll do something special. We'll all go stay in a hotel by the sea."

Year after year, Manuel put a little money in the bank. His daughters got
20 married and moved to the city. Sofia married Ruiz, and they had two children, a girl and a boy. Lucinda married Carlos, and they had a girl. On weekends, Sofia and Lucinda often went back to the village with their children. The children liked the village, and they loved Manuel and Maria. They played in the garden with the dog and the cat. They went up the mountain with Manuel to get flowers and fruit.
25 Maria cooked big meals for them and made them warm clothes.

When Manuel was 65, he stopped working. Now he did not go to the city every week. He stayed in the village with his wife. He worked in the garden, and he took care of his fruit trees. He walked a lot in the mountains, and sometimes he sat with his friends in the café. They drank coffee, talked, and played cards. He still
30 got money every month from the government, and he still put a little money in the bank.

"Soon I'll tell Maria and the girls about my money," he thought. "And next summer we'll all go to the seaside."

But Manuel and Maria always had lots of things to do. There was the house
35 and the garden, the dog and the cat, and the grandchildren. They went to school in the city now. But sometimes they were sick, and sometimes there was no school. Then they stayed with Manuel and Maria.

One day, Manuel's wife didn't feel very well. She went to bed, and Manuel called the doctor. The doctor said it was nothing. But after a week, Maria still
40 didn't feel well. The doctor sent her to the hospital in the city. The hospital doctors did some tests. They told the family she was very sick. Manuel, Lucinda, and Sofia stayed with her night and day in the hospital. A month went by and Maria didn't get better. The doctors then said she was going to die.

Sofia and Lucinda drove her home to the village. She lived for a few more
45 weeks. Manuel stayed with her all the time. The daughters came often. And then, one day, she said goodbye to Manuel and she died.

Lucinda and Sofia stayed with Manuel for a week after that. They put away all Maria's clothes and things. They cleaned the house and cooked. Then they went back to the city, back to their families and their jobs.

50 Now Manuel was alone. Some women in the village said, "We can help you in the house. We can make dinner for you and wash your clothes. You don't have to pay us very much."

Manuel said no, he didn't want help. He didn't want other women in his house. He also didn't want to pay these women. He had money in the bank, but it
55 wasn't for the village women.

Some years went by. Manuel learned how to cook and how to wash his clothes. His house was always clean, and his garden was full of fruit and vegetables. Now his grandchildren didn't come very often because they had to study on the weekends. His daughters said, "Why don't you come live in the city with us?"

60 But Manuel didn't want to leave his home. Now he didn't want to go to the seaside. He didn't want to go away without Maria. He was 77 years old. On some days, he felt very old and tired. Then he liked to sit in his garden with his cat and his dog. Of course, these were not the same cat and dog. They were the first cat's and dog's children's children!

65 One day, Manuel looked at the cat and the dog. Now they were old, too. The dog never barked, and the cat never ran after mice. "We're all old now," Manuel said to them. "We're all going to die before long. Then who will get my money? I don't want the bank to have it! I must go and get it."

So, one morning, Manuel went to the bank. He asked for all his money. The
70 bank manager came and talked to Manuel. He said, "What are you going to do with this money? You have $30,000. You can't walk home with $30,000!"

Manuel said, "It's my money. I can do what I want." He put the money in a bag and went home. At home, he put the money under his bed. He didn't want people to find it. But that night he didn't sleep well. When the cat came into his
75 room, he said, "Who's that?" and jumped out of bed.

"This is no good," he said. "I can't live with all this money in my house."

In the morning, he went out to the garden. He made a big hole under a plum tree. He put the bag of money in the hole. He put dirt back in the hole, and he put grass on top. Every day, he looked at that place under the plum tree. He often
80 thought about the money, and he thought about his daughters and grandchildren. But the money stayed under the plum tree, because there was a problem. Manuel couldn't decide about the money. He had $30,000, and he had two daughters. He could give $15,000 to each daughter. But Sofia had two children and Lucinda had only one. So that was not good. He could give money only to the grandchildren.
85 He could give them $10,000 each. But that meant no money for his daughters. He couldn't do that!

The winter went by. Spring came and there were lots of flowers on the plum tree. Manuel still couldn't decide about his money. Summer came and Manuel's garden was full of fruit and vegetables. But the plum tree had very few plums and
90 those plums were not sweet.

"I think the tree is telling me something," said Manuel. "Money must not stay in a hole in the ground."

He telephoned his daughters. "Please come this weekend," he said. "I have something important to tell you."

95 Sofia and Lucinda came on Friday evening with their families. Sofia's daughter, Yolanda, was now 20 years old and her son, Pablo, was 17. Lucinda's daughter, Julia, was 18. Yolanda was a university student. She wanted to be a doctor. Pablo and Julia were high school students. Pablo wanted to be a writer and Julia wanted to be a police officer.

100 At dinner that evening, Manuel said nothing about the money. Lucinda looked at Sofia, and Sofia looked at her father. They talked about the city and the government. They talked about the village and the garden. Yolanda, Pablo, and Julia went for a walk around the village. "What's he going to tell us?" they asked. But Manuel told them nothing that evening, and they all went to bed.

105   At breakfast the next morning, Manuel said, "Now it's day. Now I'm ready. Come with me to the garden."

Manuel went to the plum tree and stopped. "I'm getting old," he said. "I'm going to die before long. I want to give you something."

He took the grass away from the hole. He took out the dirt. "Oh, no!" he cried.

110   "What is it?" asked his daughters.

"Look!" he said. "Look at that hole. It's empty!" Manuel sat down on the grass. "Who took it?" he cried. "Who took it?"

"Who took what?" asked Sofia and Lucinda.

"My money!" said Manuel.

115   "Your money?" they asked. "Why did you put money in the ground? Money must stay in the bank!"

"I didn't want the bank to have my money. It was my money," said Manuel. "I wanted to give it to you."

"How much was it?" asked Sofia.

120   "$30,000," said Manuel.

"$30,000!" said Sofia and Lucinda. "You put all that money in a hole in the ground?"

Poor Manuel. He sat on the ground with his head in his hands.

"We must go to the police!" said Ruiz.

125   "Yes, we must tell them," said Carlos. "Maybe they can find the thief."

So Ruiz, Carlos, Sofia, and Lucinda ran to the police. Yolanda, Pablo, and Julia stayed with Manuel in the garden. Julia looked in the hole. She put her hands in and pulled out some very small pieces of paper.

"Look!" she said. "Look at these."

130   "Pieces of money!" said Pablo.

"Why in little pieces?" asked Yolanda. "What kind of thief does that?"

"I think there were many thieves," said Julia.

"Why do you say that?" asked Pablo.

"There were many small thieves," said Julia.

135   "Children!" said Yolanda. "That's terrible! Village children!"

"No, not children," said Julia. "Very, very small thieves. They *ate* the money."

"What do you mean?" asked Pablo.

"Look in the hole," said Julia. "Do you see those little black things? What makes little black things? What eats paper?"

140   "Mice!!!" said Pablo and Yolanda.

"Yes, mice," said Julia.

Manuel looked up. "It's true," he said. "There are lots of mice. The cat is old and she doesn't run after them now."

Manuel looked at Yolanda, Pablo, and Julia. "I'm very sorry," he said. "I wanted

145   to give you that money. I wanted to send you to the seaside. I wanted . . ." He stopped.

The cat came out and sat down near Manuel. She was black and white and very fat.

"Where were you?" said Julia to the cat. "Why weren't you out here at work?"

150   "Meow!" said the cat.

"Were you asleep in the house?" asked Julia.

"Meow," said the cat.

Then Pablo started to laugh. "Think about it," he said. "$30,000! Those mice ate $30,000!"

155   Yolanda and Julia also started to laugh.

"What are the police going to do?" said Pablo. "Take the mice to jail?"

Yolanda, Pablo, and Julia laughed more and more. They fell on the ground laughing.

Manuel looked at them. He thought, "How can they laugh? That was years of
160 work, that money."

He listened to his grandchildren, still laughing and talking. And then he thought, "Maybe they're right. Why cry? I can't get the money back now."

And he smiled sadly at the cat.

Write new words here.

_____

_____

_____

_____

UNIT **3** Reading Books for Pleasure

Looking for a Pleasure Reading Book

How to find a book you'll like:

1. Read the title (name) of the book.

2. Look at the picture on the cover and read the back of the book.
   What is it about? Is it interesting?

3. Read the first page of the book.
   Find out how many words are new for you.

   No new words → This book may be too easy for you.

   1–5 new words → This book is right for you.

   6 or more new words → This book may be difficult for you.

Example:

Back cover   Front cover

1. What is the title of this book? _____

2. Look at the front and back covers of the book.

   What is this book about? _____

   Is it interesting to you? _____

3. Read the first page of *Simon and the Spy*.

Simon Simple is at the station. He is going on a train.
There are policemen at the station. There are
policemen on the trains. They are all working very hard.
"Why are the police here?" Simon asks a man. "Look,"
the man says. Simon looks at the man's newspaper.
"Do you know this man?" he reads. *"He's a* **spy**! *Find
him! Stop him! Catch him!"*

How many words are new for you? _____

Is this book right for you? _____

Talk about this book with another student. Are your answers the same?

Talking about Pleasure Reading Books

After you read a book, talk about it. Talk to your friends and to your
teacher. Here are some questions to ask and answer about books:

What is the book about?

Who is the author (writer)?

Who is in the story?

Where are they?

Do you like this book? Why or why not?

Learn More New Words from Your Pleasure Reading Book

After you read, write the new words in your notebook. (See page 124.) Write the word and write the sentence (or sentences) around the word. Next, write the meaning of the word (in English or your language). Then, check the meaning with your teacher or in the dictionary.

Example:

○	*Simon and the Spy,* page 1:
	New word: *station*
	Sentences: *Simon Simple is at the station. He is going on a train.*
	Meaning: *a place to get on a train*
	Check the meaning. Is it correct? *yes*

Writing about Pleasure Reading Books

Pleasure Reading Report

Write a report about your pleasure reading book. Copy this form on a piece of paper and then fill it in. Remember to draw a line under the title of the book. Then give it to your teacher.

Pleasure Reading Report

Title of book: _____

Name of author: _____

How many pages in the book? _____

What is this book about? _____

_____

_____

Is this book true? _____ Is it easy to read? _____

Do you like this book? _____ Why? _____

Is this a good book for a friend to read? _____

Why? _____

Write a Letter about Your Book

You can write about a book in a letter. Here is a letter about *Simon and the Spy*.

Dear <u>Maria</u>,

    I just read a book. I want to tell you about it. The book's title is <u>Simon and the Spy</u>. The author's name is <u>Elizabeth Laird</u>.

    This book is about <u>Simon and Samantha and how they meet a spy on a train and then on a boat</u>.

    The story is <u>very funny</u>. The book is <u>easy</u> to read.

    I <u>like</u> this book <u>very much</u> because <u>I like the ending</u>. I think you <u>should read it</u>.

                         Your friend,
                          Wang

Now write a letter about <u>your</u> pleasure reading book.

Dear _____ ,

    I just read a book. I want to tell you about it. The book's title is

_____.

    The author's name is _____.
    This book is about _____.

_____.

    The story is _____.
    The book is _____ to read.
    I _____ this book _____ because

_____.

    I think you _____.

                         Your friend,

                       _____

Pleasure Reading Book List

Make a list of your pleasure reading books here. When you write the title of a book, put a line under it.

1. Title _____

   Author _____

   Number of pages _____ Date begun _____ Date finished _____

2. Title _____

   Author _____

   Number of pages _____ Date begun _____ Date finished _____

3. Title _____

   Author _____

   Number of pages _____ Date begun _____ Date finished _____

4. Title _____

   Author _____

   Number of pages _____ Date begun _____ Date finished _____

5. Title _____

   Author _____

   Number of pages _____ Date begun _____ Date finished _____

PART 2

Comprehension Skills

UNIT 1   Scanning for Key Words

What is scanning? It's a way to read very fast. You do not read all the words. You read only the words you're looking for.

In these exercises you learn to find words quickly. Then you can read quickly. Circle the key word every time you see it in the line.

Example:

Key word

1. **read**	real	(read)	reel	raid	(read)
2. **three**	tree	there	(three)	these	trees

EXERCISE 1

Circle the key word every time you see it in the line. Work quickly.

Key word

1. **into**	onto	unto	into	intro	into
2. **been**	been	bean	born	been	barn
3. **back**	black	bark	back	bank	book
4. **must**	much	must	mist	mush	muse
5. **then**	them	then	ten	than	then
6. **way**	way	why	wax	way	wry
7. **out**	our	cut	oust	own	out
8. **all**	ail	all	awl	owe	all
9. **with**	witch	with	wish	will	wit
10. **over**	ever	aver	over	our	over

Circle the key word every time you see it in the line. Work quickly.

Key word

1. **they**	thy	they	then	them	they
2. **what**	what	when	white	what	wit
3. **down**	dawn	darn	done	dean	down
4. **may**	my	may	many	way	marry
5. **time**	twine	tine	turn	time	time
6. **would**	want	would	walked	should	world
7. **you**	you	yes	yon	you	yore
8. **also**	alas	alto	also	ails	also
9. **much**	must	mast	mush	much	munch
10. **after**	alter	altar	after	afar	otter

EXERCISE 3

Circle the key word every time you see it in the line. Work quickly.

Key word

1. **before**	baffle	belief	befriend	before	belfry
2. **which**	witch	which	winch	whisk	which
3. **was**	watt	war	was	wan	wan
4. **are**	art	arc	air	ago	are
5. **were**	were	wear	were	ware	wore

6. **about**	abound	abuse	about	abut	about
7. **there**	there	their	these	theme	three
8. **new**	now	net	sew	new	not
9. **our**	out	our	own	our	oar
10. **any**	ant	nay	awry	and	any

EXERCISE 4

Circle the key word every time you see it in the line. Work quickly.

Key word

1. **will**	wilt	wall	with	will	wild
2. **made**	made	made	make	maid	mode
3. **their**	there	these	three	their	their
4. **years**	yours	years	yarns	years	yards
5. **did**	did	die	dill	dud	dad
6. **him**	hum	him	him	ham	hem
7. **most**	moat	must	mast	mouth	most
8. **could**	cold	collect	could	called	could
9. **your**	year	your	your	yarn	yore
10. **through**	thought	though	threw	through	tough

Circle the key word every time you see it in the line. Work quickly.

Key word

1. **can**	car	cad	con	can	can
2. **two**	tow	too	to	two	too
3. **have**	hare	home	have	hive	have
4. **from**	from	form	from	farm	firm
5. **not**	not	net	nut	mat	met
6. **had**	hid	had	has	has	had
7. **more**	more	mare	mere	more	mark
8. **some**	sons	soon	some	soar	soon
9. **these**	these	three	there	their	those
10. **where**	were	where	when	where	whose
11. **for**	far	fir	fur	four	for
12. **way**	why	way	wag	way	war
13. **well**	wall	wall	well	will	welt
14. **only**	any	ugly	angle	only	onto
15. **other**	antler	other	otter	odder	other
16. **first**	forth	fist	first	first	forest
17. **such**	sick	such	sock	much	such
18. **said**	said	sail	sad	said	sale

Circle the key word every time you see it in the line. Work quickly.

Key word

1. **into**	onto	unto	into	intro	into
2. **been**	been	bean	born	bane	been
3. **back**	black	bark	back	back	book
4. **must**	much	must	mist	must	muse
5. **then**	them	then	then	than	then
6. **way**	way	why	wax	way	wry
7. **also**	alas	alto	also	ails	also
8. **much**	mulch	mast	mush	munch	much
9. **after**	alter	altar	afar	otter	after
10. **before**	baffle	belief	before	bereft	bored
11. **down**	dawn	darn	done	down	dean
12. **which**	witch	which	winch	whisk	which
13. **was**	watt	war	was	wan	wan
14. **are**	art	arc	air	ago	are
15. **were**	were	wear	ware	wore	were
16. **about**	abound	abuse	about	abut	about
17. **our**	out	our	own	our	oar
18. **any**	ant	nay	awry	and	any

Circle the key word every time you see it in the line. Work quickly.

Key word

1. **have**	hare	hove	have	hive	have
2. **from**	from	form	farm	firm	from
3. **not**	not	net	nut	mat	met
4. **their**	there	these	three	their	there
5. **more**	more	mare	mere	more	mire
6. **some**	sons	soon	some	soar	soon
7. **these**	these	three	there	their	those
8. **where**	were	where	when	where	whose
9. **time**	twine	tine	turn	time	time
10. **would**	want	would	could	should	world
11. **write**	white	writes	with	write	while
12. **also**	alas	alto	also	ails	also
13. **much**	must	mast	mush	much	munch
14. **after**	alter	altar	afar	otter	after
15. **from**	from	form	farm	firm	from
16. **not**	not	net	nut	mat	met
17. **had**	hid	hub	has	hat	had
18. **more**	more	mare	mere	more	mire

Circle the key word every time you see it in the line. Work quickly.

Key word

1. **always**	away	ways	always	asleep	always
2. **close**	clothes	close	class	clock	class
3. **fast**	fast	food	fist	fast	first
4. **grass**	gram	grass	gray	green	grass
5. **head**	hear	help	hair	here	head
6. **letter**	lesson	light	listen	letter	liter
7. **month**	many	month	mouth	money	morning
8. **near**	never	name	north	near	nose
9. **oil**	old	our	oil	one	all
10. **over**	oven	out	over	open	over
11. **ship**	self	she	shape	ship	sits
12. **says**	said	says	saying	sails	self
13. **read**	raid	red	ready	read	rain
14. **speak**	spoon	sleep	asleep	speak	street
15. **talk**	tall	tell	taxi	take	talk
16. **their**	there	them	their	then	their
17. **thanks**	thinks	thanks	thank	think	tanks
18. **story**	stony	store	story	stop	store

Circle the key word every time you see it in the line. Work quickly.

Key word

1. **ten**	tin	ton	tan	tune	ten
2. **other**	other	otter	odder	after	other
3. **saw**	sow	saw	say	sum	sew
4. **end**	end	and	odd	enter	end
5. **here**	here	hard	here	hair	hare
6. **city**	catty	cite	cost	coy	city
7. **letter**	liter	litter	letter	latter	lather
8. **would**	would	world	wailed	walled	would
9. **few**	few	foe	flew	fear	few
10. **say**	ski	say	sky	easy	soy
11. **start**	stars	stared	smart	start	skirt
12. **then**	than	thin	there	then	that
13. **time**	timed	timer	tame	time	timid
14. **them**	then	there	them	than	theme
15. **money**	many	morning	marry	movie	money
16. **work**	walk	wake	work	wall	work
17. **store**	sore	stare	story	store	shore
18. **bank**	back	bank	balk	bask	back

Exercise 10

Circle the key word every time you see it in the line. Work quickly.

Key word

1. **open**	oven	opera	pen	poem	open
2. **clock**	clock	chock	clack	click	cloak
3. **out**	oust	owed	own	our	out
4. **when**	when	where	went	whose	what
5. **like**	line	lake	lick	like	alike
6. **small**	smoke	smile	smell	small	simile
7. **boat**	boast	boot	boat	both	boat
8. **even**	ever	even	oven	seven	over
9. **clean**	clear	clan	clam	clean	clean
10. **fall**	fall	fill	fell	fault	fall
11. **tale**	talk	tall	trail	tail	tale
12. **short**	short	start	share	shore	short
13. **move**	movie	more	mare	move	moved
14. **wait**	with	wait	waist	water	want
15. **plane**	planet	plans	plane	plank	plane
16. **next**	neat	nest	next	next	text
17. **learn**	lean	lease	leery	learn	lard
18. **shop**	shop	ship	shot	shod	shed

Readers often scan for information. They don't read all the words. They read only the words they need. You can learn to scan for information in these exercises. Work quickly. Remember—you don't have to read all the words!

EXERCISE 1

Here is a newspaper ad for some pop music concerts.

A. Scan the ad and answer the questions. Work quickly.

1. Can you see Jimmy Buffet in August? _____

2. When can you see Dixie Chicks? _____

3. Who is playing on August 22? _____

4. How many concerts are in June? _____

5. Who is the star on July 4? _____

6. What time do the concerts start? _____

7. How much are the tickets for James Taylor? _____

8. What is the name of Taj Mahal's band? _____

B. Write three more questions about this ad. Then ask another student to scan for the answers.

_____?

_____?

_____?

C. Talk with another student. Ask and answer these questions.

1. Are your answers to questions 1–8 the same?

2. Do you know the music of any of the stars in this ad? Which ones?

3. Do you like any of them? Why?

4. What is your favorite kind of music?

James Taylor and his traveling band of musicians

June 28 & 29
$48, $38 Res. – $28 G.A.

Bruce Springsteen & the N.J. Band

July 4, 5, 6
$95, $60 Res. – $45 G.A.

Fleetwood Mac
*Stevie Nicks,
Lindsey Buckingham,
Mick Fleetwood,
& John McVie*

July 11
$50–$125

Jimmy Buffett and the Coral Reefer Band

July 25, 26
All seats $50

THE MUSIC ARENA

Summer Popular Artist Series
All shows start at 7:30 P.M.

Lucinda Williams & the traveling band

August 9
$35, $45 Res. – $25 G.A.

Dixie Chicks with Michelle Branch

August 16
$80, $65, $45

Cher "Living Proof Tour"

August 22, 23
$40, $80
Partial proceeds to charity

Taj Mahal & the Hula Blues Band

August 29, 30, 31
$38, $48 Res. – $20 G.A.

Classified ads are not for stores or companies. People put classified ads in the newspaper. There are many things to buy and sell in these ads. Some ads are about something lost or found. Other ads tell about classes.

A. Scan the ads and answer the questions. Work quickly.

1. How many bicycles are for sale? _____

2. What is the price of the 32" TV and DVD/VCR? _____

3. How many dogs were found? _____

4. Were any cats found? _____

5. What is the cost per hour for the house cleaner? _____

6. What is the price of English lessons in your home? _____

7. What is the telephone number for the gardener? _____

8. When does the new class for dance lessons begin? _____

9. How much is the reward for the lost keys? _____

10. Where was the violin made? _____

B. Write three more questions about the classified ads. Then ask another student to scan for the answers.

_____?

_____?

_____?

C. Talk with another student. Ask and answer these questions.

1. Are any of these ads interesting to you? Why?

2. Look at the "Lost and Found" ads. There are two ads about cats. What do you think?

3. Can you give lessons in a language? Or a sport? Or music? Tell what you can do.

Los Angeles News

Classified Ads

For Sale

Desk chair. $15. Like new. 223-3222

Dining room set, 6 chairs. Beautiful, old. $700. 342-9982

Bicycle. 1 year old. 21 speeds. $75. 663-9280

Bicycle. Man's. Good for hills. $90. 641-2398

Violin. Made in Italy. Like new. $3,000. 663-2929

32" TV and DVD/VCR. 2 years old. Must sell now. $350. 769-5055

1998 Jeep Wagon. Low miles. One owner. $2,200 or best offer. 996-8765

Lost and Found

Lost. Keys on ring. Near High St. $25 reward. Call 321-1212

Lost: Black and white cat. 2 years old. Near Green St. Please call 939-9310

Lost. Sunglasses in red case. Near School St. Reward. 773-7219

Found: Black and white cat. Green St. at City Park. 794-4582

Found: Big black dog. Small ears. Short hair. Near Flower St. 393-1974

Lost. Near University Rd. Camera in brown case. Need for my job. Reward. Please call 723-2901

Classes and Tutoring

Dance class. New class begins in May. Ten students in a class. Six weeks, $75. Call today! 525-0800

Math lessons. Tutor can help you! $15/hour. Call 566-7878

English lessons in your home. Very good teacher. $20/hour. 793-7287

Piano lessons. Ace Music School 978-3210

Learn to speak Chinese. Hong Kong teacher. $25/hour. 356-4678

Piano lessons. Teacher from Russia. Call today. 894-0759

English classes for beginners. Six students in a class. 736-2984

Home Services

House cleaner. Clean windows, floors, kitchen. $12/hour. Call Hilda Today! 978-6543

Gardener. Cut the grass, clean up leaves, plant new flowers and trees. Good worker. Gus. 688-3214

Charlie's Window Service. Broken windows? We fix them fast! 334-9876

Need a new roof? Call Ron's Roofing Co. Fast and experienced. 887-4576

Rugs and carpets cleaned. Low prices. 832-6832

Newspapers often have large ads for drugstores.

A. Scan this drugstore ad and answer the questions. Work quickly.

1. How much is the Everyday Headache Relief? _____

2. Can you find any cough syrup? What brand? _____

3. How many ounces (oz.) are in the All-Day Hair Spray? _____

4. How much is the Face Guard razor? _____

5. How many tablets are in the kids' formula Daily Vitamins? _____

6. Can you find any toothpaste? What brand? _____

7. How many kinds of razors are there? _____

8. How many things cost more than $5.00? _____

9. How many deodorants are in the ad? _____

10. How much is the Doctor's Stomach Relief?   _____

B. Write three more questions about this ad. Then ask another student to scan for the answers.

_____?

_____?

_____?

C. Talk with another student. Ask and answer these questions.

1. You are going to this drugstore. Which things do you want to buy? Why?

2. Can you find these things in other countries?

A. Scan the menu and answer the questions. Work quickly.

1. How many salads are on the menu? _____

2. How much is the chicken soup? _____

3. How many different drinks are on the menu? _____

4. How much is the fruit juice? _____

5. How many ways can you eat lobster? _____

6. Do you get french fries with the roast chicken? _____

7. What is the most expensive thing on the menu? _____

8. How many desserts are on the menu? _____

B. Write three more questions about this menu. Then ask another student to scan for the answers.

_____?

_____?

_____?

C. Talk with another student. Ask and answer these questions.

1. Did you find some new words on this menu? What are they?

2. Would you like to eat at Marie's Seaside Café?

3. Do you like everything on the menu? If not, what don't you like?

4. Which dessert on the menu do you like most?

Marie's Seaside Café

Town Harbor Shopping Center
Newburyport, Massachusetts

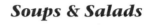

Soups & Salads

Soup of the day	$2.50
Chicken soup	$2.00
Clam chowder	$3.00
House salad	$3.50
Garden salad	$2.00
Tomato salad	$2.75

Seafood & Chicken
(served with french fries)

Fried clams	$4.50
Lobster	$9.00
Fried fish	$6.50
Fried chicken	$7.00
Roast chicken	$6.50

Sandwiches

Hamburger	$6.00
Cheese	$3.00
Egg salad	$3.00
Lobster roll	$8.50
Tuna salad	$4.50

Drinks

Tea, Coffee	$1.50
Spring water	$1.50
Fruit juice	$2.00

Desserts

Ice cream	$2.00
Chocolate cake	$2.50
Apple pie	$2.50

A. Scan the list of pleasure-reading books and answer the questions. Work quickly.

1. Who is the author of *The Psychic*? _____

2. Which book is about a 12-year-old girl? _____

3. Which story takes place in England? _____

4. Which book has 49 pages? _____

5. Which story takes place in ancient Egypt? _____

6. Who is the author of *Inspector Thackeray Arrives*? _____

7. Which book is about a man with a new job? _____

8. Which book has the most pages? _____

9. How many pages are there in *Dangerous Journey*? _____

10. Which story is about a Canadian hero? _____

B. Write three more questions about the book list. Then ask another student to scan for the answers.

_____?

_____?

_____?

C. Talk with another student. Ask and answer these questions.

1. Would you like to read any of these books?

2. Which one(s) and why?

3. What kind of books do you like most?

Books for Pleasure Reading

Alissa, by C. J. Moore. Alissa is a 12-year-old girl. She lives in a poor village. Her parents send her to work in the city. She works hard and she gets little money. Will she find a way out of this unhappy life? (16 pages)

Dangerous Journey, by Alwyn Cox. Four men are trapped in the forest. Heavy rain has turned the tracks into mud. The bridge across the river is broken. Can they get back to the camp? Can they cross the deep river to safety? (31 pages)

Everything's Different on the Job, by Penny Cameron. Vijay gets a new job selling houses. He has to learn many new skills. Then he makes a big mistake. Will he have to pay for it from his salary? (49 pages)

The Fireboy, by Stephen Rabley. Hapu lives in ancient Egypt. He works for his father, a goldsmith. One day Hapu has a wonderful idea. He will make a beautiful gold necklace for Queen Cleopatra. (15 pages)

Inspector Thackeray Arrives, by Kenneth James. Inspector Thackeray is a detective. He has to find the criminal. That's not easy, but the criminal always makes mistakes. Can you see the mistakes? Can you find the criminals? (46 pages)

The Last Photo, by Bernard Smith. Pam and Martin are visiting Cambridge for the day. Pam has a camera, and she takes a picture of Martin. The picture may help the police. (15 pages)

The Long Road, by Rod Smith. Terry Fox has cancer, and he loses one of his legs. He wants to help other people with cancer. He runs across Canada to get money for them. He runs with one good leg and a leg made of plastic. This is the story of a strong athlete—and a Canadian hero. (15 pages)

The Psychic, by Paul Victor. James Brent was a psychic. He saw things in the past, and he saw things far away. He helped the police find murderers. But one day he saw too much! (30 pages)

The Woman in Black, by Susan Hill. This story takes place in England, many years ago. Arthur Kipps is a young lawyer. He is sent to a lonely house. A woman died in the house, and he hears many strange noises. (57 pages)

Here is the table of contents for the book *Making Business Decisions*. What can you learn about this book?

A. Scan the table of contents and answer the questions. Work quickly.

1. How many units are there? _____

2. Which units are about food companies? _____

3. Which unit is about the clothing business? _____

4. Which company makes ice cream? _____

5. On what page does the unit about supermarkets begin? _____

6. Which units have a writing exercise about business letters? _____

7. Which units are about international business or trade? _____

8. Which unit is about new products? _____

B. Write three more questions about this table of contents. Then ask another student to scan for the answers.

_____?

_____?

_____?

C. Talk with another student. Ask and answer these questions.

1. Do you know the companies in the units? Which ones?

2. Is this an interesting book? Why or why not?

CONTENTS

To the Teacher vii

What does it mean to "make an inference?" It means that you guess. When you make an inference, you have some information and you guess more things from that information.

You often make inferences in your life. You can make inferences on the bus, for example. You hear two people talking. You do not know what they are talking about. But after you listen a little, you can guess what they are talking about.

Making inferences is important when you read. It can often help you understand what you are reading. Good readers, in fact, make inferences all the time. In these exercises, you can learn to make inferences.

Example:

Look at the picture and answer the questions. You must make inferences from the picture. Work with another student.

1. Where are these people? <u>*They are in an office.*</u>

2. What are their jobs? <u>*They are a businessperson and a customer.*</u>

3. What are they doing? <u>*The customer is asking about something.*</u>

4. What are they saying? <u>*She is saying, "I would like some information."*</u>

Make inferences from this picture and answer the questions. Work with another student. Then talk to some other students. Do they have the same answer?

1. Where are these people? _____

   _____

2. What are their jobs? _____

   _____

3. What are they doing? _____

   _____

4. What are they saying? _____

   _____

Make inferences from this picture and answer the questions. Work with another student. Then talk to some other students. Do they have the same answers?

1. Where are these people? _____

_____

2. What are their jobs? _____

_____

3. What are they doing? _____

_____

4. What are they saying? _____

_____

These riddles are about food. Make inferences to answer the questions. Then talk to another student. Do you have the same answers?

1. It's brown.

   You can drink it.

   You can put milk or sugar in it.

   It isn't tea.

   What is it? *coffee* _____

2. First it's red.

   After you cook it, it's brown.

   What is it? _____

3. It's orange.

   It's often long and thin.

   Sometimes you cook it and sometimes you don't.

   What is it? _____

4. It's white.

   It's sweet.

   You can put it in coffee or tea.

   You often put it in cakes.

   What is it? _____

(continued on next page)

5. It's white.
   It's not sweet.
   You can put it on meat or vegetables.
   You don't put it in coffee.

   What is it? _____

6. It's white or brown.
   You can make sandwiches with it.
   You can put butter on it.
   You can eat it alone.

   What is it? _____

7. It can be red, green, or yellow.
   It comes from a tree.
   You can eat it anytime.
   You can cook it, too.

   What is it? _____

8. It's white.
   You must cook it.
   You can put butter on it.
   You can eat it with meat or vegetables.

   What is it? _____

These riddles are about animals. Make inferences to answer the questions. Then talk to another student. Do you have the same answers?

1. It can jump far.

   It sleeps a lot.

   It makes a soft noise when it is happy.

   Many people have them in their homes.

   What is it? _____

2. It lives in most places around the world.

   It is small and gray.

   It has a long tail.

   Some people are afraid of it.

   What is it? _____

3. It lives on farms.

   It eats grass.

   It usually stays in groups.

   People make warm clothes from its hair.

   What is it? _____

4. It's very big.

   It lives in the ocean.

   It needs to come up to get air.

   The baby drinks milk from its mother.

   What is it? _____

5. It's very small and it can fly.

   It's not very clean.

   It goes on food.

   People try to kill it.

   What is it? _____

These riddles are about places. Make inferences to answer the questions. Then talk to another student. Do you have the same answers?

1. It's a building.

   It's for children.

   Some adults are there, too.

   The children are studying.

   The adults are teaching.

   What is it? _____

2. It's in a building.

   There are lots of tables.

   Some people are eating.

   Some people are cooking.

   Some people are bringing food to the tables.

   What is it? _____

3. It's not in a building.

   It has trees and it sometimes has flowers.

   Children like to play there.

   Dogs like to run there.

   People like to sit there.

   What is it? _____

4. It's in a building.

   People sit and work there.

   Other people stand and wait.

   Some want to get money.

   Some want to give money.

   What is it? _____

5. It's outside in the yard.

   It's small.

   It has a door but no windows.

   Something lives there.

   Cats do not like to go near it.

   What is it? _____

These riddles are about jobs. Make inferences to answer the questions. Then talk to another student. Do you have the same answers?

1. He sees lots of children.

   Some children are sick.

   He helps them get well.

   He listens to the mothers and fathers.

   He tells them what to do.

   What is his job? _____

2. Sometimes she sits at a desk.

   Sometimes she walks through the store.

   She answers some people's questions.

   She helps other people at work.

   She wants lots of people in the store.

   What is her job? _____

3. He works in a tall building.

   His office is on top.

   He has meetings in restaurants.

   He makes telephone calls in his car.

   He has an airplane, too.

   What is his job? _____

4. She goes to many places around the world.

   Sometimes there are wars or dangerous weather.

   She talks to the people in these places.

   Then she tells their stories to the people at home.

   Many people watch her on TV.

   What is her job? _____

5. She sits down all day.

   But she moves around the city.

   She goes to the same places every day.

   She sees many different people.

   They pay to go with her.

   What is her job? _____

Often, you have to make inferences to understand stories. Here is part of a story. Read it and then make inferences to answer the questions. Then talk to another student. Do you have the same answers?

The sun is going down. Jonas cannot find the road. He listens to the river and stays near it.

What is that? Jonas hears something. He listens. A man is near. A man is calling. A man wants help!

"Where are you?" Jonas calls.

"Here! Come here! Help me!" the man answers.

Jonas looks behind a big stone. "Harry!" he says. "What are you doing here?"

"I'm running from Bernie and Pete," Harry says. "But my leg is bad. I can't go on. Bernie and Pete are looking for me. They're angry. There isn't any gold in this river."

"What?" Jonas says. "But you . . . in the bar . . . ."

"It's not in the water," Harry says. "It's here. Look." He brings out the bags of gold.

1. Where are these people? _____

2. What is Harry doing? _____

3. Why are Bernie and Pete angry? _____

_____

4. What did Harry say in the bar? _____

_____

Here is part of a story. Read it and then make inferences to answer the questions. Then talk with another student. Do you have the same answers?

Four days later, Jenny and Blue Sky are making the beds. Suddenly they hear something. Two men are shouting. Jenny looks out of the window. She can see Jack Crane and her father in front of the farmhouse. Jack Crane's face is very red.

"*Do* it!" he shouts.

"No, I'm not going to!" Sam shouts back. "It's Sunday and I don't work on Sundays. *You* do it!"

Jenny runs downstairs and out of the house. There is a strong wind and it is raining.

"What's happening?" she asks her father.

"We're leaving in the morning," Sam answers. He is walking very fast. Jenny looks at him.

"But . . . how are we going to *eat*? We don't have any money."

Sam does not answer. His eyes are cold and hard.

1. Where are these people? _____

2. What does Jack Crane want? _____

3. Why are Sam's eyes cold and hard? _____

   _____

4. What does Jenny think? _____

   _____

Here is part of a story. Read it and then make inferences to answer the questions. Then talk to another student. Do you have the same answers?

Leaping Larry says, "We want to see the island."

"All right," says Duncan. "We can go in my boat."

Duncan, Larry, and Roxanne get into Duncan's boat. Jock jumps in, too. Roxanne is carrying Bobo.

Duncan takes them around the island. The sun is shining and it's a beautiful day. But Roxanne isn't happy.

"What do you do all day?" she asks Duncan.

"Well," says Duncan, "I go for walks and I fish. And sometimes I go swimming."

"Is that all?" Roxanne asks.

"Well," says Duncan, "I'm also writing a book."

"A book!" says Roxanne. "What about?"

"About Lana," says Duncan.

"Oh," says Roxanne. "That isn't very exciting."

"Listen, honey," says Larry. "We can make the island exciting. We can have pop concerts here. It's just fine for concerts. Hundreds of people can come!"

Duncan looks at Jock. Jock looks at Duncan.

"Pop concerts!" they think. "Oh, no!"

1. Where are these people? _____

2. Where does Duncan live? _____

3. Does Larry like the island? Why or why not? _____

_____

4. What does Duncan think? _____

_____

Here is part of a story. Read it and then make inferences to answer the questions. Then talk to another student. Do you have the same answers?

I walked over to the bed. On it, face down, was a photograph. Who was the picture of? I was afraid to look. I took the photograph in my hand and slowly turned it over.

"What the . . . ?" I shouted.

"What is it?" said Susan. "Can I see?"

"You can," I said, "but it isn't good!"

I gave her the photo. Susan looked at it, and jumped back. "But it's you and me!" she said.

"I know," I said, and looked again.

It was Susan and me. Down at the sea.

"That man!" said Susan excitedly. "He was there. It's *his* photo!"

Suddenly, we heard a noise. The door opened. And there he was, the man with my face. And he had a gun in his hand.

"Very clever!" he said quietly. "It was me."

He shut the door.

"Don't move," he said. "Or I'll shoot."

I looked at the man in horror. I wasn't afraid of his gun—I was afraid of his face! He had my nose, my mouth, my ears, my hair . . . .

1. Where are these people? _____

2. Why is the narrator ("I") afraid to look? _____

3. Why did the man take a picture of "Susan and me"? _____

    _____

4. Why did he have the same face? _____

    _____

UNIT 4

Understanding Sentences

When you read English, you must understand English sentences. These exercises will help you learn how to find the important parts of sentences.

EXERCISE 1

Make sentences. Draw a line from A to B. Then write sentences on the lines below.

A	B
1. Suki is drinking	a bus.
2. Carol is cooking	in a chair.
3. Sam is driving	near the door.
4. Sergio is sitting	coffee.
5. Laura is standing	a book.
6. Don Pablo is reading	dinner.

Write the sentences here.

1. _Suki is drinking coffee._____

2. _____

3. _____

4. _____

5. _____

6. _____

Talk to another student. Are your sentences the same?

Make sentences. Draw a line from A to B to C. Then write sentences on the lines below.

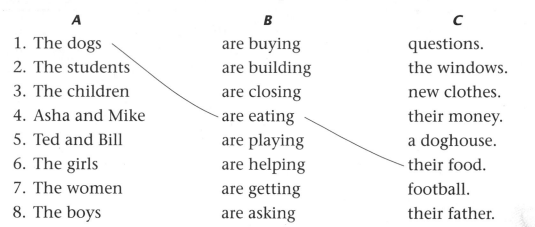

A	**B**	**C**
1. The dogs	are buying	questions.
2. The students	are building	the windows.
3. The children	are closing	new clothes.
4. Asha and Mike	are eating	their money.
5. Ted and Bill	are playing	a doghouse.
6. The girls	are helping	their food.
7. The women	are getting	football.
8. The boys	are asking	their father.

Write the sentences here.

1. *The dogs are eating their food.* _____

2. _____

3. _____

4. _____

5. _____

6. _____

7. _____

8. _____

Talk to another student. Are your sentences the same?

Write adjectives in the blanks. Then write new sentences on the lines below. You can use the adjectives in the box or you can use other adjectives.

young	beautiful	cold	slow	green
new	angry	hot	fast	white
old	happy	dry	tall	brown
bad	big	sick	red	yellow
good	small	sad	blue	black

1. The __young__ man is driving a __green__ car.

   The young man is driving a green car.

2. The _____ girl is eating a _____ sandwich.

   _____

3. A _____ dog is looking for the _____ cat.

   _____

4. A _____ bird lives in that _____ tree.

   _____

5. The _____ teacher is talking to a _____ girl.

   _____

6. This _____ book is about _____ cities.

   _____

7. _____ children do not like _____ animals.

   _____

8. The _____ woman is giving a _____ flower to a _____man.

   _____

Talk to another student. Are your sentences the same?

A. Make sentences. Draw a line from A to B. Add an adjective and then write the sentences on the lines below.

A	B
1. The horse	are talking to the _____ teacher.
2. That house	doesn't like _____ dresses.
3. My sister	is eating a ____big____ apple.
4. Simon's brother	cook _____ meals in the evening.
5. Some restaurants	has _____ windows.
6. The students	has _____ friends.
7. The airplane	is flying through a _____ cloud.
8. Mr. and Mrs. Jenkins	have _____ flowers on the tables.

1. *The horse is eating a big apple.* _____

2. _____

3. _____

4. _____

5. _____

6. _____

7. _____

8. _____

B. Write some new sentences. Put an adjective in every sentence.

1. The horse _____.

2. That house _____.

3. My sister _____.

4. Simon's brother _____.

5. Some restaurants _____.

6. The students _____.

7. The airplane _____.

8. Mr. and Mrs. Jenkins _____.

C. Talk to another student. Are your sentences the same?

Write adverbs in the blanks. Then write the sentences on the lines below. You can use the adverbs in the box or you can use other adverbs.

always	sometimes	fast	well	often
never	usually	slowly	badly	quickly

1. I _____*often*_____ read the newspaper in the morning.

   _I often read the newspaper in the morning._____

2. I read English _____.

   _____

3. My family _____ goes to restaurants.

   _____

4. My father _____ washes the windows.

   _____

5. I do my homework _____.

   _____

6. My friend rides a bicycle _____.

   _____

7. I _____ go to the bank on Saturday.

   _____

8. My mother drives a car _____.

   _____

Talk to another student. Are your sentences the same?

A. Make sentences. Draw a line from A to B to C. Then write the sentences on the line below.

A	B	C
1. A tall man	is learning	at night.
2. That old dog	is waiting	down the street.
3. Our English class	wakes up often	for you.
4. My baby sister	is walking fast	the cat's food.
5. The new doctor	always eats	to read well.

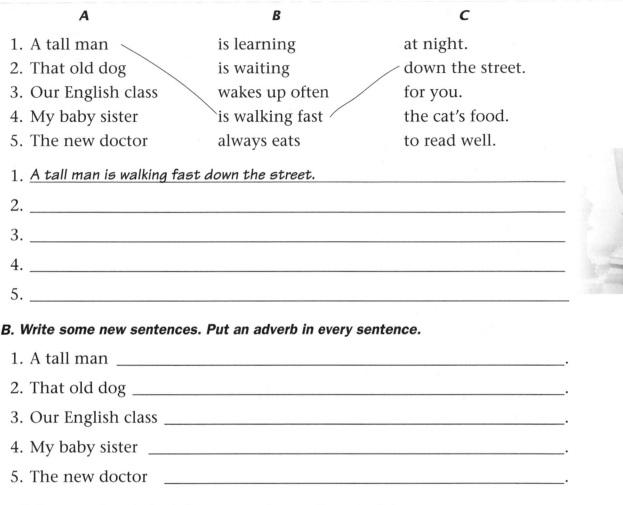

1. _A tall man is walking fast down the street._

2. _____

3. _____

4. _____

5. _____

B. Write some new sentences. Put an adverb in every sentence.

1. A tall man _____.

2. That old dog _____.

3. Our English class _____.

4. My baby sister _____.

5. The new doctor _____.

C. Talk to another student. Are your sentences the same?

A. Make sentences. Draw a line from A to B to C. Then write the sentences on the lines below.

A	B	C
1. Those girls	sometimes play	meat.
2. Some people	always eat	with the boys.
3. My parents	watch television	in that room.
4. Those men	don't eat	much free time.
5. Three children	never have	very quickly.

1. _____

2. _____

3. _____

4. _____

5. _____

B. Write some new sentences. Put an adverb in every sentence.

1. Those girls _____.

2. Some people _____.

3. My parents _____.

4. Those men _____.

5. Three children _____.

C. Talk to another student. Are your sentences the same?

Read the pronouns in the box below. Look for these pronouns in the sentences. Draw a line under every pronoun.

Subject pronouns:	I	you	he	she	it	we	they
Object pronouns:	me	you	him	her	it	us	them
Possessive pronouns:	my	your	his	her	its	our	their

1. Liz has two little girls. <u>Their</u> names are Anna and Piper. <u>They</u> go to

   school on the school bus.

2. Hattie works at a small restaurant. She usually works in the morning. The restaurant is often very busy then. It is full of people eating breakfast.

3. Dan is a teacher in Los Angeles. He teaches people to read. His students are not children. They are men and women who do not know how to read.

4. Bob likes making bread. He makes many kinds of bread. All of his bread is very good, but his French bread is the best. It is just like the bread in France.

5. Rocky loves to go to the movies with her friends. Every Friday night, she goes to see a movie with them. Last Friday, she saw an Italian movie. She said it was very good.

6. Carol has two jobs. Her first job is at a college. She teaches English as a second language. Her second job is at home. She writes books for little children.

7. Alex built a new house for his family. He worked on the house for two years. Now it is finished. He and his family moved into the house last week.

8. Ken loves to grow flowers. His favorite flowers are roses. He has lots of roses in his back yard. Sometimes he gives beautiful roses to his friends.

9. Steven is a doctor in a small hospital. His patients are poor people. Often they do not have much money. So he sees them for free and he gives them free medicine.

10. Paul moved from Boston, in the United States, to Santiago, in Chile. He is very far from home. But he has lots of new friends in Santiago. They are very kind to him and take him to visit interesting places in Santiago.

Talk to another student. Did you underline the same words?

Write the correct pronoun in each blank. Work with another student.

Life in the Chi Family

Mike Chi and _____*his*_____ wife, Laura, have a fruit and vegetable store
             (1)

on Main Street. _____*They*_____ work in the store with _____*their*_____ son, Tony.
          (2)   **(3)**

Tony goes to school in the morning. In the afternoon, _____ helps
                                                        (4)

_____ parents in the store.
    (5)

Mike and Laura get up very early in the morning. Mike has a big truck.

He drives _____ to the city market, and _____ buys fruit and
              (6)   **(7)**

vegetables for the store. Laura washes the floor and the windows of the

store. She gets _____ ready for the day. The Chi family lives in an
              (8)

apartment near _____ store. Laura goes home first in the afternoon.
                  (9)

_____ goes shopping and cooks dinner. At 7:00, Mike closes the
    (10)

store. _____ and Tony go home for dinner. After dinner, Tony does
          (11)

_____ homework and _____ parents watch TV and read.
    (12)   **(13)**

Talk to two other students. Are your pronouns the same?

Key Words in Sentences

Good readers in English look for the key words in a sentence. The key words are the subject and the verb. The subject tells who or what the sentence is about. The verb tells what the subject does.

Example:

> Yoko lives in Rosebud, New Jersey.
> **S**   **V**

The subject of this sentence is *Yoko*. The sentence is about Yoko.

The verb in this sentence is *lives*.

EXERCISE 10

Read each sentence. Work with another student. Underline the <u>subject</u> and the <u>verb</u>. Then write S under the subject and V under the verb.

1. She listens to music with her friends.

2. Yoko also plays music on the piano.

3. Every week she goes to New York for piano lessons.

4. She rides the bus with her friend Lucy.

5. Lucy takes violin lessons in New York.

6. Yoko's piano teacher is Mr. Bernstein.

7. He is a famous pianist.

8. Yoko and Lucy want to be famous, too.

9. They play music together.

10. Sometimes they give concerts for their friends.

Talk to two other students. Did you underline the same words?

Read each sentence. Work with another student. Underline the <u>subject</u> and the <u>verb</u>. Then write S under the subject and V under the verb.

1. Asha Sachdev works as a film star in India.

2. Many Indian people like to see her films.

3. They all know and love Asha's face.

4. People see her face on the walls.

5. Big pictures of her face are all around the city.

6. Films are big business in India.

7. Every year Indians make about 900 films.

8. These films always have some sad parts and some happy parts.

9. Every film has a beautiful woman and a love story.

10. Music is an important part of every Indian movie.

Talk to two other students. Did you underline the same words?

EXERCISE 12

Read each sentence. Work with another student. Underline the <u>subject</u> and the <u>verb</u>. Then write S under the subject and V under the verb.

1. Ho Kwangliang lives in Taichung, Taiwan.

2. He is the president of Hung Ming Enterprises.

3. His company makes parts of shoes.

4. Many shoe companies buy parts of shoes from Ho's company.

5. He does business with famous companies in the United States and Europe.

6. Ho's company makes $25 million every year.

7. One hundred people work for Hung Ming Enterprises.

8. They work in eight different buildings.

9. Ho plans to open a new company in Shanghai, China.

10. That company will make parts of shoes, too.

Talk to two other students. Did you underline the same words?

UNIT 5 Looking for Topics

What is a "topic"? A topic tells what something is about.

Good readers always look for the topic when they read. Then they can understand and remember what they read.

There are two kinds of topics. One kind of topic is the name of a group of things. Another kind of topic is the name of a thing with many parts.

Topics That Are Names of Groups

EXERCISE 1

What is the topic of these pictures?

1. Topic: *hats*

2. Topic _____

3. Topic _____

4. Topic: _____

Find the topic word in each group of words and circle it. Then write the topic on the line. Work with another student.

1. Topic: *color*

   red   yellow   blue   orange   brown   (color)

2. Topic: _____

   pop   music   rock   country   classical   jazz

3. Topic: _____

   animals   cats   dogs   horses   pigs   elephants

4. Topic: _____

   brother   son   father   men   grandfather   uncle

5. Topic: _____

   apple   banana   orange   fruit   pear   mango

6. Topic: _____

   morning   night   times of day   evening   afternoon   noon

7. Topic: _____

   walks   talks   sleeps   builds   verbs   begins

8. Topic: _____

   shirts   clothes   dresses   pants   coats   socks

9. Topic: _____

   hotels   hospitals   banks   schools   buildings   theaters

10. Topic: _____

    Japan   Brazil   China   France   Korea   countries

Find the topic word in each group of words and circle it. Then write the topic on the line. Work with another student.

1. Topic: _____

   breakfast   dinner   supper   meals   lunch   snack

2. Topic: _____

   aunt   sister   women   mother   girlfriend   daughter

3. Topic: _____

   books   magazines   newspapers   letters   reading material

4. Topic: _____

   soda   coffee   orange juice   drinks   tea   water

5. Topic: _____

   teacher   doctor   taxi driver   jobs   singer   secretary

6. Topic: _____

   table   furniture   chair   sofa   desk   bed

7. Topic: _____

   bus   car   plane   taxi   transportation   train

8. Topic: _____

   fork   spoon   knife   cup   tableware   bowl

9. Topic: _____

   basketball   football   sports   tennis   baseball   Ping Pong

10. Topic: _____

   dining room   restaurant   coffee shop   café   eating places   snack bar

Topics That Name Things with Many Parts

These things are all part of something. What is it?

1. Topic: *computer*

2. Topic: _____

3. Topic: _____

Find the topic word in each group of words and circle it. Then write the topic on the line. Work with another student.

1. Topic: _____

   husband   family   son   daughter   cousin   wife

2. Topic: _____

   trees   flowers   grass   birds   bushes   garden

3. Topic: _____

   arms   legs   neck   body   head   feet

4. Topic: _____

   students   books   teacher   pens   paper   classroom

5. Topic: _____

   nose   head   mouth   ears   hair   eyes

6. Topic: _____

   wheels   doors   windows   seats   car   engine

7. Topic: _____

   minute   second   hour   day   time   week

8. Topic: _____

   building   roof   walls   doors   stairs   windows

9. Topic: _____

   apartment   bedroom   living room   kitchen   bathroom   hall

10. Topic: _____

    desk   computer   bookcase   office   chair   telephone

More Practice with Topics

In Exercises 6–12, you can find both kinds of topics. Some topics are names of a group. Other topics name something with many parts.

EXERCISE 6

Find a topic for each group of words. Write it on the line. Work with another student.

people who work with money	people who work outside
people who work with people	people who work with their hands
people who work in government	people who work in a hospital
people who often work at night	people who make music

1. Topic: *people who work in government*

   mayor   president   governor   prime minister   commissioner

2. Topic: _____

   taxi driver   doctor   baker   police officer   telephone operator

3. Topic: _____

   doctor   orderly   nurse   technician   surgeon

4. Topic: _____

   cellist   pianist   violinist   trumpeter   soprano

5. Topic: _____

   teacher   doctor   nurse   lawyer   professor

6. Topic: _____

   artist   gardener   cook   nurse   pianist

7. Topic: _____

   banker   cashier   accountant   gambler   economist

8. Topic: _____

   gardener   football player   police officer   farmer   road worker

Find a topic for each group of words. Write it on the line. Work with another student.

games played with a ball	parts of a computer
things used for cooking	parts of a library
things used in school	parts of a hospital
things in a handbag	parts of a supermarket

1. Topic: _____

   meats   bakery   check-out   fish   fresh vegetables

2. Topic: _____

   frying pan   soup pot   spoon   egg beater   mixing bowl

3. Topic: _____

   wallet   keys   glasses   comb   cell phone

4. Topic: _____

   reference section   information desk   fiction   non-fiction   catalog

5. Topic: _____

   football   tennis   golf   cricket   croquet

6. Topic: _____

   emergency room   intensive care   nursery   pharmacy   waiting room

7. Topic: _____

   books   pens   maps   desks   notebooks

8. Topic: _____

   keyboard   monitor   disk   speakers   mouse

1. This group of words has two topics. Write the topics and write the words under them. Work with another student.

candy	orange	mango	apple	cookies
cake	chocolate	ice cream	banana	grapefruit

Topic 1: _fruit_ _____

Topic 2: _sweets_ _____

_____   _____

_____   _____

_____   _____

_____   _____

2. This group of words has two topics. Write the topics and write the words under them. Work with another student.

chapter	adjective	page	table of contents	verb
noun	pronoun	adverb	paragraph	title

Topic 1: _____

Topic 2: _____

_____   _____

_____   _____

_____   _____

_____   _____

3. Think of some words for these topics. Then look at another student's words. Do you have any of the same words?

Topic 1: _favorite foods_ _____

Topic 2: _beautiful cities_ _____

_____   _____

_____   _____

_____   _____

_____   _____

Think of a topic for each group of words and write it on the line. Then think of one more word for each topic and write it. Work with another student.

1. Top<u>ic: *park*</u>

 trees   bushes   birds   grass   fountain   <u>*flowers*</u>

2. Topic: _____

 chicken   pork   lamb   beef   rabbit   _____

3. Topic: _____

 meat   cheese   fruit   bread   vegetables   _____

4. Topic: _____

 car   bus   boat   train   bicycle   _____

5. Topic: _____

 soda   tea   milk   coffee   water   _____

6. Topic: _____

 uncle   brother   father   grandfather   grandson   _____

7. Topic: _____

 morning   evening   midnight   night   noon   _____

8. Topic: _____

 history   fable   news article   poem   novel   _____

9. Topic: _____

 nine   fifteen   three   thirty   twenty-one   _____

10. Topic: _____

 feet   legs   arms   head   neck   _____

Think of a topic for each group of words and write it on the line. Then think of one more word for each topic and write it. Work with another student.

1. Topic: _____

    green   red   yellow   orange   _____

2. Topic: _____

    cherries   bananas   apples   pears   _____

3. Topic: _____

    table   chairs   oven   sink   _____

4. Topic: _____

    four   eight   twelve   sixteen   _____

5. Topic: _____

    Paris   London   Berlin   Stockholm   _____

6. Topic: _____

    cake   balloons   candles   gifts   _____

7. Topic _____

    ocean   river   lake   pond   _____

8. Topic: _____

    cat   dog   goldfish   mouse   _____

9. Topic: _____

    guitarist   drummer   pianist   singer   _____

10. Topic: _____

    dollar   euro   pound   yen   _____

Write the topic. One word does not belong to the topic. Cross out that word. Work with another student.

1. Topic: <u>*rooms in a house*</u>

   bedroom   living room   kitchen   ~~wall~~   bathroom

2. Topic: _____

   nose   ears   eyes   mouth   hand

3. Topic: _____

   England   New York   France   Mexico   China

4. Topic: _____

   cup   hat   plate   glass   spoon

5. Topic: _____

   runs   cries   laughs   days   talks

6. Topic: _____

   new   beautiful   clean   garden   happy

7. Topic: _____

   wheels   windows   doors   desk   engine

8. Topic: _____

   city   hour   day   week   month

9. Topic: _____

   music   food   dancing   read   drinks

10. Topic: _____

    Canada   Los Angeles   Boston   New York   Chicago

Write the topic. One word does not belong to the topic. Cross out that word. Work with another student.

1. Topic: _____

   juice   cereal   toast   coffee   ice cream

2. Topic: _____

   plane   bus   bicycle   boat   house

3. Topic: _____

   coat   hat   dress   clock   shirt

4. Topic: _____

   cake   ice cream   hamburger   pie   cookies

5. Topic: _____

   sister   aunt   mother   grandfather   daughter

6. Topic: _____

   dollar   yen   peso   euro   bank

7. Topic: _____

   twenty   fifteen   seventeen   thirty   ten

8. Topic: _____

   France   Italy   Brazil   Germany   Spain

9. Topic: _____

   lions   panthers   elephants   tigers   dogs

10. Topic: _____

    March   Winter   November   May   June

What is a paragraph?

A paragraph is a group of sentences about one topic. There is usually one sentence that tells you the topic. All the other sentences tell more about the topic. Good readers look for the topic that way.

Example:

1. Is this a good paragraph?

   Every morning, Susan Powers eats a big breakfast. She eats two eggs, one slice of bread, and a banana. She drinks a glass of orange juice and a big cup of tea. Susan says she is ready to go to work after a good breakfast.

   (Yes)   No

2. Is this a good paragraph?

   Every morning, Susan Powers eats a big breakfast. She works in a bank in New York. Many people work at the bank. Some people go shopping before work. Others go shopping in the morning. On rainy days, they all bring their umbrellas to work.

   Yes   (No)

   Number 1 is a good paragraph. All of the sentences are about one topic: Susan's breakfast. Number 2 is not a good paragraph. The sentences are about many different topics.

Remember

- A good paragraph has one topic.

- All the sentences are about that topic.

Read about New York City. Are these all good paragraphs? Is each paragraph about one topic?

New York City

1. Visitors come to New York from all over the world. In New York, they can go to the museums. They can do business on Wall Street, and they can go to the theaters. People like the many good restaurants and nightclubs in New York. They also love shopping for special things in big stores and small shops. Visitors can have a good time in New York.

Is this a good paragraph? _____

2. Central Park is a very big park in New York. It is usually full of people. The Bronx Zoo is usually full of visitors. Many taxis drive down Fifth Avenue. Young families bring their children to play there. Other people like to run or ride their bicycles by the river. You can meet friends at a small restaurant.

Is this a good paragraph? _____

3. New York is one big city. But the city has many different parts. In some parts, most of the people are rich. In some parts, most of the people are poor. Students and working people live in other parts. And in some parts, there are many people from the same country. For example, a part of New York is called Little Italy, and another part is called Chinatown.

Is this a good paragraph? _____

4. Chinatown is in the southern part of New York City. Most of the people in Chinatown are Chinese. Street signs and shop signs are written in Chinese. Many other New Yorkers like to go there. They like to eat at the Chinese restaurants. They like to shop in Chinese stores.

Is this a good paragraph? _____

5. New York City is home to more than 8,000,000 (eight million) people. Another big city is Los Angeles, California. Near Los Angeles, people can visit Hollywood and look for movie stars. There are two airports in New York. The tallest building in the United States is in Chicago.

Is this a good paragraph? _____

Talk to another student. Are your answers the same?

EXERCISE 2

Read these groups of sentences. Are they all good paragraphs? Is each paragraph about one topic?

Music

1. Many people like listening to music. Some people go to concerts. They like to watch people make music. Other people listen to music at home. They can listen to tapes or CDs. They can also listen to music on MTV or on the computer.

Is this a good paragraph? _____

2. There are many famous opera singers. Luciano Pavarotti is a famous opera singer. He's from Modena, Italy. Modena is a beautiful small city in the north of Italy. You can find lots of good cheese and wine in Italy. Italian people eat lots of pasta.

Is this a good paragraph? _____

3. Jazz music began in America. Many famous rock stars are English. In Boston you can listen to lots of good classical music. Bjork is a very popular pop singer. She is from Iceland. She also sings her songs in movies. John Williams writes music for the movies. He wrote the music for the movie about Harry Potter.

Is this a good paragraph? _____

4. Young people often listen to loud music. They listen to loud music on their headphones. They go to very loud concerts. All this loud music is bad for their ears. In fact, many young people cannot hear very well.

Is this a good paragraph? _____

5. Music can help people in many ways. It can help people who are sick. The music makes them forget they are sick. It can also help people who are unhappy. It makes them feel better about their lives. Music is like medicine for many people. But it is better than medicine because it is free.

Is this a good paragraph? _____

Talk to another student. Are your answers the same?

EXERCISE 3

Turn to Unit 4, Exercise 11, page 86.

1. Write sentences 1–5 as a paragraph.

Topic: Asha Sachdev, Indian film star

_____

_____

_____

_____

_____

_____

_____

_____

2. Write sentences 6–10 as a paragraph.

Topic: Films in India

_____

_____

_____

_____

_____

_____

_____

_____

Talk to another student. Are your paragraphs the same?

Turn to Unit 4, Exercise 12, page 86. Write the sentences as a paragraph.

Topic: Ho Kwangliang's shoe companies

_____

_____

_____

_____

_____

_____

_____

_____

Talk to another student. Are your paragraphs the same?

Read the paragraphs below. Ask these questions: What is this paragraph about? What is the topic? Then circle the best topic for each paragraph.

Computers and the Internet

Example:

People use computers in many jobs these days. Writers use computers to write books or articles. With computers, they can print their work fast. Then they can read it and make changes and print it again. Musicians use computers to write music. They play the music on computers, and then print it out. Business people use computers, too. They use them to write letters and reports. They also use them to do math and work on their business. Scientists also use computers to do lots of math fast. And they use computers to make pictures of things. Then they can study the pictures to understand something better.

What is the best topic?

a. How business people use computers

b. Ways people use computers for work

c. Different kinds of jobs these days

Choice a, "How business people use computers," is not a good topic. It tells us about only part of the paragraph.

Choice b, "Ways people use computers for work," is a good topic. It tells us about everything in the paragraph.

Choice c, "Different kinds of jobs these days," is not a good topic. It is too big for the paragraph. This paragraph only tells about computers at work. It doesn't tell about work in other ways.

1. Do you have an e-mail address? Millions of people around the world have e-mail addresses. With e-mail, you can "talk" with people from Montevideo to Kyoto. It does not cost very much, and it is fast. E-mail helps many people with their work. Other people use it for fun. They talk with their families or with their friends. They also make friends with new people that they "meet" on the Internet.

a. Telephone communication

b. How e-mail helps at work

c. How people use e-mail

2. If you want to use e-mail, you need a connection to the Internet. You can connect to the Internet through a telephone line or by cable or satellite. You write your e-mail message on the computer and you give the computer an address. Then you tell the computer to send the message to that address. Your computer sends it to a big computer, called a server. The server sends your letter to another server. That server sends it to the e-mail address that you gave it. That is how e-mail works.

a. How e-mail works

b. How the Internet talks to computers

c. How a telephone line works

3. Many people use the Internet to get information. They get information from library web sites, for example. On the web sites they can read newspapers, magazines, and books. People also look at web sites for businesses. A company's web site tells about the things a company makes, does, or sells. And people use the Internet for travel information. They can find out about flights and hotels from travel web sites. They can also print out maps and pictures.

a. Reading newspapers on the Internet

b. Using the Internet to get information

c. Getting information for your work

4. These days, people can do a lot of business on the Internet. For example, you don't have to go to the bank. You can do your banking on the Internet. You may want to buy tickets for a concert. You can do that on the Internet, too. You can also do lots of shopping on the Internet—for food, clothes, books, and other things. You choose what you want from the pictures on the Internet. Then you buy it with your credit card and it comes to your house.

a. Doing business on the Internet

b. Shopping on the Internet

c. The Internet today

Talk to another student. Are your answers the same?

EXERCISE 6

Circle the best topic for each paragraph.

A Special Sport

1. Swimming, bicycling, and running are three very popular sports. Some people like to do all three sports in one race. They can do all three in a triathlon race. *Triathlon* means "three sports." In a triathlon, the people swim for a mile (1.6 km). Then they have to ride a bicycle for about 10 miles (16 km). And then they have to run for 3 miles (4.8 km). You must be a very strong person to win a triathlon!

a. What people do in a triathlon

b. Popular sports today

c. Swimming in a triathlon

2. The men and women in triathlons are called triathletes. Triathletes must work hard all year to get ready. Every day, they run and swim and ride their bicycles. They must also do special exercises for their bodies. After many months of work, they are ready for a race. There are many races in many countries. One famous triathlon is the Ironman race in Hawaii. Another is the Noosa race in Australia. Triathletes come to these races from all over the world.

a. The Ironman race

b. Races in many countries

c. Triathletes and triathlons

3. Karen Smyers and Mark Allen are two famous triathletes. Karen Smyers is from the United States. She gets ready for triathlons all year, and

she goes to many races. That is her job. The Nike company gives her money to live. Mark Allen is also a full-time triathlete, and he is also from the United States. Karen and Mark won women's and men's triathlons in many different countries. They also were the winners in the Ironman race in Hawaii.

a. The Ironman race

b. Triathletes in the United States

c. Two famous triathletes

Talk to another student. Are your answers the same?

Write a topic for each paragraph. Your topic must fit the paragraph. It must not be too big or too small.

Central America

1. Central America is not large. It is much smaller than South America or North America. It is only about 420,000 square miles (700,000 square km). That is about the size of Texas. But Central America has many different kinds of land. There are tall mountains made by volcanoes. There are large lakes, small lakes, and many rivers. There are dry places with few plants. There are very wet places with lots of plants. There is a lot of coastline, where the land meets the sea. And there are many islands.

Topic: _____

2. For scientists, Central America is a good place to study many kinds of animals. Central America is like a bridge between North and South America. Long ago, animals moved into Central America from the north and the south. They found good places to live there and they stayed. Today, these many different kinds of animals live together. Other kinds of animals live in Central America part of the year. Birds and butterflies, for example, fly to North America every spring. Then they return to Central America in the fall.

Topic: _____

3. The first people arrived in Central America about 18,000 years ago. They found lots of food and good places to live. Over the years, the number of people grew, and they moved into all parts of Central America. By 1492, there were about 7,680,000 people living there. They spoke 62 different languages. Some lived in small villages. Others, like the Maya, lived in

cities. Then the Europeans arrived. In a very few years, 90 percent of the people in Central America died. Some were killed by the Europeans, but most of them died from diseases.

Topic: _____

Talk to another student. Are your answers the same?

EXERCISE 8

Write a topic for each paragraph.

Diamonds

1. There are diamonds in Africa, Australia, Russia, and Canada. In most places, they are deep underground. People have to dig far down to get them. In some places in Africa, diamonds are not underground. They are on the ground or in rivers. But it is not easy to find them. Very few people find a diamond and become rich.

Topic: _____

2. Why are diamonds so expensive? First of all, they are a very hard kind of stone. They are used to cut other kinds of stone or metal. Diamonds are also very beautiful. In many places in the world, they have a special meaning, too. They are something special that you give to someone special. So, in India and in the United States and many other countries, diamonds mean love. But, of course, they also mean money. A diamond on your finger means you are rich.

Topic: _____

3. Diamonds are beautiful, but terrible, too. They are terrible because people do terrible things to get them. People kill and fight wars over diamonds. This happened in the past in India. And it is happening these days in Africa. The civil war in Sierra Leone happened partly because of diamonds. Diamonds are also one reason for the fighting in other countries, too. Diamonds mean more money for the armies. More money means more guns and more fighting. People lose their homes and die because of diamonds.

Topic: _____

Talk to another student. Are your answers the same?

There is a sentence missing from each paragraph in this exercise. The missing sentences are in the box. Write the correct sentence in each paragraph. Then write the topic.

> - He writes books about different places, so he has to go to those places.
> - We see through their eyes, and we learn what they are thinking and feeling.
> - We can almost see the Irish countryside and hear the people speaking.

Writers in the English Language

1. Edna O'Brien lives in England, but she is Irish. She writes stories and books about Irish people. Some of her stories are about life in Ireland in the past and others are about Ireland today. They are always very real.

   _____

   _____ They are also very true to life—

   sometimes very funny and sometimes sad. *The Country Girls* and *Time and Tide* are two of O'Brien's books.

   Topic: _____

2. Thomas Keneally is an Australian writer. He lives in Sydney with his family. But often he is not at home. _____

   _____.

   Keneally's most famous book is about Nazi Germany during World War II. It tells the story of about 1,000 Jewish people and a man named Schindler. Schindler helped these people live through those terrible times. Keneally went to Germany and many other countries to talk to people about Schindler. This book, *Schindler's List,* was made into a movie.

   Topic: _____

3. Toni Morrison is an African-American writer. She often writes about African-American women. She tells about their lives and about the terrible things that happen to them. In Morrison's books we learn a lot about these women. _____

_____

In 1993, Morrison won the Nobel Prize for Literature. Two of her most famous books are *Beloved* and *Jazz*.

Topic: _____

Talk to another student. Are your answers the same?

EXERCISE 10

In each paragraph there is one extra sentence. It is not about the topic. Find the sentence and cross it out. Then write the topic.

Example:

Hobbies

In-line skating is a very popular new sport. People in many countries around the world go in-line skating. In-line skates go on your feet like roller skates and ice skates. They have little wheels, all in a line. When you are in-line skating, you have to be careful. ~~It is also a good idea to ride your bicycle.~~ At first, you should go slowly. You should not go on streets with lots of cars or people. And you should always wear special in-line skating clothes.

Topic: *In-line skating*

The sentence "It is also a good idea to ride your bicycle." is not about in-line skating. So it is crossed out.

1. In his free time, Jeff loves to go bicycling. After many hours in the office, he wants exercise. So on weekends he goes for long bicycle rides. He works just a few miles from his home. Sometimes he rides his bicycle for a few hours and sometimes he rides all day. Some of his friends also ride bicycles. They often ride their bicycles together. The doctor says Jeff is very healthy and has very strong legs.

Topic: _____

2. On summer days, Liz works in her garden. She has some flowers and lots of vegetables. She likes the flowers, but she doesn't work with them a lot. She works most of the time with the vegetables, and she also likes to cook them. Liz likes going to the movies with her friends. She does not eat meat, so she eats lots of her vegetables. She says they are much better than the vegetables from the store.

Topic: _____

3. Mike loves to cook. He cooks all kinds of dishes, but his favorite dishes are desserts. He says cooking is very relaxing. When he is working in the kitchen, he thinks only about cooking. He doesn't think about work or about bad things. He can bake big, beautiful cakes with fruit or with chocolate. Children must not eat a lot of chocolate every day. On Saturdays, Mike has lots of time for cooking. He makes a very good dinner and a special dessert for his family.

Topic: _____

Talk to another student. Are your answers the same?

A. Here are two topics. A sentence for each topic is already there. Find the other sentences for each topic in the box. Write them on the lines after the first sentence. (You can change the order later to make good paragraphs.) Work with another student.

- Milk is another healthy drink.
- Doctors say it is bad for your stomach and your head.
- Many people drink Coca-Cola, but it is not good for you.
- It is very good for children and also for women.
- A little coffee is okay, but lots of coffee is bad.
- Orange juice is one of these healthy drinks.
- Some doctors think this is the way to a healthy life.
- It has lots of sugar, so it is bad for your teeth.
- So drink lots of orange juice and milk!
- Another drink that can be bad for you is coffee.

Topic 1: Drinks that are good for your health

Some kinds of drinks are very good for your health.

_____

_____

_____

_____

_____

Topic 2: Drinks that are not good for your health

Some popular drinks are not good for your health.

_____

_____

_____

_____

_____

B. Look again at the sentences for each topic. Rewrite the sentences in the right order. Make a good paragraph.

Paragraph 1

_____

_____

_____

_____

_____

_____

_____

_____

Paragraph 2

_____

_____

_____

_____

_____

_____

_____

_____

Talk to two other students. Are your paragraphs the same?

Write a paragraph with five or six sentences in it. Write about one of these topics.
Remember to write all of the sentences about the same topic.

A job I'd like to have *or* My job

A nice place to visit

A special person in my life

My favorite teacher

My favorite book *or* My favorite movie

_____

_____

_____

_____

_____

_____

_____

_____

_____

_____

_____

_____

Read your paragraph aloud to another student. Ask him or her these questions:

Is this a good paragraph?

Why or why not?

PART 3

Vocabulary Building

It is important to notice the parts of words. Many words in English have parts that are the same. You can learn these parts. Then it is easy to read new words.

Example:

You are reading a letter that has a new word, *brook*.

> Dear Adam,
>
>   Please come to visit me. I have a new house in a small town. There is a *brook* in the town. It is a nice place to swim and go fishing.
>
> Your friend,
Yoshi

The word *brook* begins with **br**. What other English word begins with **br**?

brother

The word *brook* ends with **ook**. What other word ends with **ook**?

book

Read the two parts (**br** and **ook**) together: "brook"

EXERCISE 1

Read each list of words. Circle the words that begin with the same letter as the key word.

Example:

Key word

back	(be)	(but)	(by)	tack	had	(been)

Key word

1. **f**or	first	far	fall	tall	fun	sun
2. **m**ore	most	much	some	must	now	were
3. **w**ere	way	was	here	well	there	will
4. **y**ou	yes	years	way	your	my	you

5. **d**id	do	had	down	dad	kid	door
6. **t**ime	to	town	down	two	him	mine
7. **s**o	some	do	no	such	said	say
8. **h**e	has	me	have	help	her	be

Talk to another student. Did you circle the same words?

EXERCISE 2

Read each list of words. Circle the words that begin with the same letter as the key word.

Key word

1. **k**ind	kid	keep	find	key	kill	bill
2. **g**o	get	gone	done	give	do	good
3. **l**ike	large	lake	bike	little	take	life
4. **p**oor	put	pig	door	book	pan	piano
5. **n**ow	next	not	who	down	new	won
6. **b**ut	before	out	been	out	be	back
7. **r**un	sun	rain	right	man	river	road
8. **s**uch	much	said	must	some	see	sad

Talk to another student. Did you circle the same words?

EXERCISE 3

Read each list of words. Circle the words that begin with the same letters as the key word.

Example:

Key word

| **th**is | (these) | (then) | (there) | time | two | (them) |

Key word

| 1. **wh**at | when | where | which | well | would | who |
| 2. **th**at | then | the | two | this | their | time |

(continued on next page)

3. **sm**all	smart	some	smell	snake	smile	smoke
4. **fr**om	fry	for	front	freeze	them	friend
5. **gr**een	grass	great	gone	give	gray	grand
6. **bl**ack	blue	back	blow	bat	blind	blood
7. **st**op	stay	stand	store	sand	say	star
8. **sh**op	she	sheet	sheep	say	ship	snap

Talk to another student. Did you circle the same words?

EXERCISE 4

Read each list of words. Circle the words that begin with the same letters as the key word.

Key word

1. **br**own	bring	bridge	back	black	bread	down
2. **cl**ass	clock	call	cloud	can	could	close
3. **sl**eep	slip	slam	ship	seep	slap	slack
4. **th**ank	think	bank	this	that	tank	them
5. **ch**ickens	chair	chain	children	clean	cheap	could
6. **pl**ease	play	plan	pull	plan	plot	peas
7. **dr**ink	dress	dream	down	drag	dip	drip
8. **sp**eak	spell	sleep	spend	park	special	speed

Talk to another student. Did you circle the same words?

EXERCISE 5

Read each list of words. Circle the words that end with the same letter or letters as the key word.

Example:

Key word

bl**ack**   back   (track)   (tack)   bank   (sack)

Key word

1. **can**   tan   man   ran   cat   ban

2. wh**en**   even   seven   why   men   then

3. mu**ch**   such   must   touch   church   which

4. m**y**   by   sky   me   try   buy

5. fir**st**   from   forest   last   best   most

6. sai**d**   red   says   bed   head   did

7. sa**t**   bat   sit   at   am   that

8. fo**r**   her   of   your   our   year

Talk to another student. Did you circle the same words?

EXERCISE 6

Read each list of words. Circle the words that end with the same letters as the key word.

Key word

1. we**re**   are   there   was   more   before   war

2. d**ay**   say   may   dog   gay   hay   ray

3. aft**er**   over   brother   also   sister   letter   often

4. t**all**   small   tell   mall   mat   call   ball

5. b**ook**   bake   cook   look   bank   took   hook

6. m**ake**   bake   made   lake   cake   take   mail

7. w**ill**   bill   hill   wall   mill   wild   fill

8. n**ame**   game   same   some   tame   fame   noon

Talk to another student. Did you circle the same words?

These words have two parts. The first part is the root word. The second part is the suffix. Find the suffix for each group of words. Then write the root words.

Example:

worker = work + -er

Suffix: *er*_____

Root word: *work*_____

worker   teacher   helper   driver   farmer

Suffix: *-er*_____

Root words: *work, teach, help, drive, farm*_____

1. sleeping   thinking   standing   working   looking
   Suffix: _____
   Root words: _____

2. player   buyer   owner   talker   washer
   Suffix: _____
   Root words: _____

3. sadness   happiness   friendliness   goodness   sleepiness
   Suffix: _____
   Root words: _____

4. swimming   playing   going   driving   farming
   Suffix: _____
   Root words: _____

5. helpful   careful   beautiful   playful   useful
   Suffix: _____
   Root words: _____

6. careless   homeless   friendless   helpless   childless
   Suffix: _____
   Root words: _____

7. gladly   friendly   manly   slowly   yearly

Suffix: _____

Root words: _____

8. eater   thinker   swimmer   listener   seller

Suffix: _____

Root words: _____

Talk to another student. Did you find the same suffixes? Do you have the same root words?

EXERCISE 8

A. Look for some words with the suffix -ing in the fables and stories in Part 1, Units 1 and 2. Make a list of words with the suffix -ing. Then write the root word.

Words with -ing	Root words
1. *walking*	*walk*
2. _____	_____
3. _____	_____
4. _____	_____
5. _____	_____
6. _____	_____
7. _____	_____
8. _____	_____

Talk to another student. Do you have the same answers?

B. Look in the fables and stories in Part 1 of this book. Find words with the suffixes -er, -less, and -ly. Write the suffixes and the root words.

Suffix: *-er*

Root words: _____

Suffix: *-less*

Root words: _____

Suffix *-ly*

Root words: _____

Talk to another student. Did you find the same words?

Making a Vocabulary List

Learn new words every week. It is important to write a list of new words. You can remember them much better that way. Here is a good way to make a vocabulary list.

- Write the new word. Say each letter as you write it. Be sure the spelling is correct.
- Write the sentence (or sentences) around the word from your reading.
- Write the meaning of the new word in English or in your own language.
- Check the meaning with your teacher or in the dictionary.

Example:

New word: _bridge_

Sentences: _They come to a river with a bridge. Some people are on the bridge._

Meaning: _Something that goes across a river._

Check the meaning with your teacher or in the dictionary. Is it correct? _yes_

A. Look back at the fables and stories in Part 1. Choose 10 of the new words you found and write the words, sentences, and meanings below. Then check the meanings.

1. a. **New word:** _____

   b. Sentence(s): _____

   _____

   c. Meaning: _____

   d. Check the meaning. Is it correct? _____

2. a. **New word:** _____

   b. Sentence(s): _____

   _____

   c. Meaning: _____

   d. Check the meaning. Is it correct? _____

3. a. **New word:** _____

   b. Sentence(s): _____

   _____

   c. Meaning: _____

   d. Check the meaning. Is it correct? _____

4. a. **New word:** _____

   b. Sentence(s): _____

   _____

   c. Meaning: _____

   d. Check the meaning. Is it correct? _____

5. a. **New word:** _____

   b. Sentence(s): _____

   _____

   c. Meaning: _____

   d. Check the meaning. Is it correct? _____

6. a. **New word:** _____

   b. Sentence(s): _____

   _____

   c. Meaning: _____

   d. Check the meaning. Is it correct? _____

7. a. **New word:** _____

   b. Sentence(s): _____

   _____

   c. Meaning: _____

   d. Check the meaning. Is it correct? _____

8. a. **New word:** _____

   b. Sentence(s): _____

   _____

   c. Meaning: _____

   d. Check the meaning. Is it correct? _____

9. a. **New word:** _____

   b. Sentence(s): _____

   _____

   c. Meaning: _____

   d. Check the meaning. Is it correct? _____

10. a. **New word:** _____

   b. Sentence(s): _____

   _____

   c. Meaning: _____

   d. Check the meaning. Is it correct? _____

B. Get a small notebook for your vocabulary list. Every week look back at your pleasure reading. Write some new words in your notebook. First, write the date. Then write the new word, the sentence(s), and the meaning.

Learning the Words on Your Vocabulary List

New Words Quiz. Write 10 words from your vocabulary list. Do not look back at the meanings in your notebook! Can you remember the meanings? Write them here.

New Words Quiz   **Date:** _____

New word   *Meaning*

1. _____   _____

                          _____

2. _____   _____

                          _____

3. _____   _____

                          _____

4. _____   _____

                          _____

5. _____   _____

                          _____

6. _____   _____

                          _____

7. _____   _____

                          _____

8. _____   _____

                          _____

9. _____   _____

                          _____

10. _____   _____

                          _____

Are these meanings correct? Look back at your notebook and see. Look again at the words from last week. Look at the words from the weeks before. Do you know them now? Do a New Words Quiz every week.

New Words Quiz   **Date:** _____

New word   *Meaning*

1. _____   _____

                                           _____

2. _____   _____

                                           _____

3. _____   _____

                                           _____

4. _____   _____

                                           _____

5. _____   _____

                                           _____

6. _____   _____

                                           _____

7. _____   _____

                                           _____

8. _____   _____

                                           _____

9. _____   _____

                                           _____

10. _____   _____

                                           _____

New Words Quiz   **Date:** _____

    New word   *Meaning*

1. _____   _____

    _____

2. _____   _____

    _____

3. _____   _____

    _____

4. _____   _____

    _____

5. _____   _____

    _____

6. _____   _____

    _____

7. _____   _____

    _____

8. _____   _____

    _____

9. _____   _____

    _____

10. _____   _____

    _____

New Words Quiz   **Date:** _____

New word   *Meaning*

1. _____   _____

                        _____

2. _____   _____

                        _____

3. _____   _____

                        _____

4. _____   _____

                        _____

5. _____   _____

                        _____

6. _____   _____

                        _____

7. _____   _____

                        _____

8. _____   _____

                        _____

9. _____   _____

                        _____

10. _____   _____

                        _____

Remember: Do a New Words Quiz every week.

UNIT 3 The 100 Words

Do you know about the "100 words"? You see these words very often when you read in English. You know many of them already. Good readers know them all very well. They read the words very quickly. They do not have to stop and think. This way, good readers can think more about the ideas. They understand better.

Now you can learn the 100 words. Here is the list of words.

a	from	next	these
about	had	no	they
after	has	not	this
all	have	now	through
also	he	of	time
an	her	on	to
and	here	one	two
any	him	only	up
are	I	or	was
as	if	other	way
at	in	our	we
back	into	out	well
be	is	over	were
been	it	said	what
before	its	she	when
but	like	so	where
by	many	some	which
can	may	such	who
could	me	than	will
did	more	that	with
do	most	the	would
down	much	their	years
even	must	them	yes
first	my	then	you
for	new	there	your

Learn to spell the 100 words. Then you can read them quickly. Write in the missing letters. Then write the word.

1. d o _____ do _____
2. w _ s _____
3. b _ t _____
4. t h _ _____
5. w i l_ _____
6. y o _ _____
7. w _ y _____
8. o _ t _____
9. w _ _____
10. s _ _ e _____
11. s u _ h _____
12. w _ t h _____

13. l i k _ _____
14. o n l _ _____
15. m _ n y _____
16. b _ e n _____
17. u _ _____
18. b a _ k _____
19. y o _ r _____
20. a b _ u t _____
21. w o u l _ _____
22. a _ t e r _____
23. w h e _ e _____
24. b e _ o r e _____

Write in the missing letters. Then write the word.

1. s_ _____
2. m _ r e _____
3. b e e _ _____
4. a _ l _____
5. w e l _ _____
6. t h _ m _____
7. y _ s _____
8. i _ t o _____
9. w _ r e _____
10. s _ i d _____
11. e v _ n _____
12. d _ w _ _____

13. t i m _ _____
14. o _ e r _____
15. f _ o m _____
16. m _ y _____
17. c o u _ _ _____
18. w h i c _ _____
19. y e _ r s _____
20. t h e i _ _____
21. n e x _ _____
22. t _ e s e _____
23. w h e _ _____
24. t h _ y _____

Write in the missing letters. Then write the word. (Some have more than one right answer.)

1. y o u _ _____

2. w _ a t _____

3. h _ v e _____

4. n e _ _____

5. s a i _ _____

6. t h _ n _____

7. t h _ t _____

8. c a _ _____

9. h _ r e _____

10. a _ y _____

11. t h i _ _____

12. t _ m _ _____

13. t _ _ _____

14. w _ _ t _____

15. e _ _ n _____

16. m _ s t _____

17. w o _ _ _ _____

18. t _ _ m _____

19. o _ r _____

20. a b _ _ t _____

21. s h _ _____

22. w e _ _ _____

23. o _ h _ r _____

24. d _ _ n _____

Write in the missing letters. Then write the word. (Some have more than one right answer.)

1. _ s _____

2. _ id _____

3. _ i m _____

4. _ o _____

5. _ e r e _____

6. _ i m e _____

7. _ h e n _____

8. _ a n y _____

9. _ a y _____

10. _ u t _____

11. _ o w _____

12. _ y _____

13. _ h i c h _____

14. _ h e i r _____

15. _ t h e r _____

16. _ h e r e _____

Write in the missing letters. Then write the word. (Some have more than one right answer.)

1. w e _ _ _____

2. w _ o _____

3. n _ t _____

4. t h _ _ _____

5. b a _ _ _____

6. y o _ _____

7. e v _ _ _____

8. o _ r _____

9. w _ _____

10. s a _ d _____

11. a l _ _ _____

12. t _ m _ _____

13. d o w _ _____

14. o n l _ _____

15. m _ n y _____

16. f _ r s _ _____

17. n e _ _____

18. w h _ _ _ _____

19. y _ _ r _____

20. a b _ _ t _____

21. w o u _ _ _____

22. a _ t _ r _____

23. o _ _ r _____

24. t h e _ _ _____

Some of the 100 words are in this puzzle. You can read words across (like this →) or down (like this ↓).

Find these words and circle them:

after ✓	are	did	had	me	of	they
all	before	down	he	most	or	to
also	but	even	him	my	our	up
and	by	for	in	new	some	way
any	can	from	may	no	then	your

N	A	F	T	E	R	F	R	O	M
E	L	Z	O	H	A	D	B	U	T
W	S	R	N	I	N	A	L	L	H
D	O	W	N	M	A	Y	A	R	E
I	M	O	S	T	N	O	C	A	N
D	E	V	E	N	D	U	O	F	A
B	E	F	O	R	E	R	X	T	N
L	Z	O	U	R	S	T	H	E	Y
W	L	R	P	H	A	I	M	O	O
A	N	E	R	E	L	N	E	B	Y
Y	T	O	M	Y	S	O	O	R	C

Many of the 100 words are in this puzzle. Find 20 words and circle them. Then write them below the puzzle.

T	H	R	O	U	G	H	L	N	O
I	A	B	O	U	T	O	W	O	N
M	S	Y	O	U	H	V	H	W	I
E	V	E	N	B	E	E	E	B	Y
R	N	S	I	T	S	R	R	E	T
B	E	F	O	R	E	Z	E	I	F
A	N	Y	F	A	B	O	U	T	I
C	A	N	T	W	O	U	L	D	R
K	N	O	O	N	A	T	H	A	S
M	O	S	T	O	T	H	E	R	T

_____   _____

_____   _____

_____   _____

_____   _____

_____   _____

_____   _____

_____   _____

_____   _____

_____   _____

_____   _____

Talk to another student about his or her words and your words. Are they the same?

Some of the 100 words are in these sentences. Write in the missing letters in those words.

1. **Allen:** W *o u l d* yo_ lik_ so_e milk w_ _h y_u_ coffee?

   Lynne: N _, thanks. _ l_k_ black coffee.

2. **Suha:** Wh_t _s yo_r name?

   Yuki: M_ name i_ Yuki.

   Suha: I_ th_t a Japanese name?

   Yuki: Ye_, i_ _s.

3. **Pat:** Whe_e a_e yo_ fr_ _?

   Stan: I'm fr_ _ Texas.

   Pat: D_ yo_ li_ _ t_ ride horses?

   Stan: N_. No_ al_ Texans li_e t_ ride horses!

4. **Stefan:** D_ yo_ li_ _ t_ read love stories?

   Milly: N_, I don't. I l_ _e to read ab_ _ _ _
   science an_ computers. Th_y're m_ _h
   m_r_ interesting.

5. **Craig:** Wh_n di_ y_ _ call yo_r mother?

   Ivan: I called h_ _ be_ _ _ _ lunch.

   Craig: W_s sh_ a_ home?

6. **Ivan:** No, s_ _ w_s still _t work.

   Craig: Wh_ _e does s_ _ work?

   Ivan: A_ _ bank i_ New York.

   Craig: Does s_ _ come b_ck home f_ _ lunch?

   Ivan: N_, s_ _ eats lunch a_ work.

Read the sentences. Fill in the letters. Then write the words in the puzzle.

Across

1. Do you have m_ book?

4. I w_ _ _d like some tea.

6. W_ have no class on Sunday.

7. Will she come b_ _ _ today?

9. He's going to Chicago n_ _ _ Tuesday.

10. Where a_ _ you from?

11. I did n_ _ go to school today.

13. Ask Tom and Helen for a ride. T_ _ _ have a car.

Down

2. I want to talk to y_ _.

3. She d_ _ all the work yesterday.

5. Do you l _ _ _ orange juice?

6. W_ _ _ is the class party?

8. Sunday comes a _ _ _ _ Saturday.

10. He likes to read a_ _ _ _ cars.

12. Will you b_ home today?

A. Read the sentences. Fill in the letters. Then write the words in the puzzle.

Across

2. Take the stairs d _ _ _ to the first floor.
4. Do you know t _ _ _ _ names?
6. He h _ _ two cats in his apartment.
7. I think s _ _ is a new student.
9. She saw m _ _ _ beautiful places.
14. I found the book t _ _ _ _, on the desk.
15. I don't know. I w _ _ _ ask her.
16. That is s _ _ _ a pretty name.

Down

1. Ben doesn't have a _ _ dogs.
2. When d _ _ Stella go to Japan?
3. Do you like cats o _ dogs?
4. He calls t _ _ _ Boris and Gleb.
5. Her name i _ Tanya.
6. When did she come h _ _ _?
8. Stella was i _ Japan last year.
10. I like a _ _ animals.
11. Y _ _, I'd like to meet her.
12. What is h _ _ name?
13. Ivan has t _ _ dogs.
14. Who is t _ _ _ tall girl?

B. You can make two stories using the sentences in part A. Copy the sentences below.

Story 1

_____

_____

_____

_____

_____

_____

_____

Story 2

_____

_____

_____

_____

_____

_____

_____

Talk to another student. Are your stories the same?

What is context? It's the sentence or sentences around a word. The context can tell you a lot about a word.

These exercises can help you learn about context. Some words are missing in each story. You must use the context to find the right words.

First read the story. Think about the context for each missing word. Then look for the right words.

Example:

Mara Milvaney is 36 years old. Mara and her family live in a small _____ in Australia.

What is the missing word?

horse	meat	girl	town	yard

The missing word is *town*. It is the only word that is good for this context. A family does not live in a horse, a meat, a girl, or a yard.

EXERCISE 1

Read the story. Write the words in the right places.

horse	meat	girl	~~town~~	yard

Mara Milvaney is 36 years old. Mara and her family live in a small _town_ in Australia. Mara and her husband, Dan, have three children, two boys and a _____. They live in a small house with a large _____. The children like animals very much. The family has three cats, two dogs, and a _____.

Mara and Dan have a sheep farm. They sell the young sheep for _____. People in Europe and the United States buy the meat. Mara also sells the sheep's wool for clothes. Australian wool goes to many countries.

Talk to another student. Are your words the same?

EXERCISE 2

Read the story. Write the words in the right places.

fisherman	garden	evening	boat	sea

Malcolm Morris is 29 years old. He lives in Charlotteville, Tobago. Tobago is a small country in the Caribbean Sea. Malcolm's town is near the _____. There are few cars in this town, but there are many boats.

Malcolm is a _____. Every morning he goes out early in his _____ and catches some fish. In the afternoon he works in his vegetable _____. He eats lots of fish and vegetables. He also sells some fish in another town. In the _____ he sometimes works with the other fishermen. They often work on their boats. Sometimes he sits in a café with his friends. They like to talk about fishing and life.

Talk to another student. Are your words the same?

Read the story. Write the words in the right places. This time there is an extra word!

daughter	housework	yard	bread	friends	store

Lidia Mazza is 89 years old. She lives in Bazzano, a small town in Italy. She lives in the same house with her daughter, her daughter's daughter, and her daughter's daughter's _____! Her son and his children live in the next town.

Mrs. Mazza does not work in the house now. Her daughter does the _____. Mrs. Mazza often works in the garden. She loves her flowers and vegetables. She also goes out to the _____ every morning. Sometimes she walks and sometimes she rides her bicycle. She buys milk and _____ for her family. She talks with the people in the store or with _____ on the street. She likes to tell them about her family.

Talk to another student. Are your words the same?

Read the story. Write the words in the right places. There is an extra word!

| planes | family | countries | company | war | soldiers |

Diem Tam Tranh is 58 years old. He lives in Ho Chi Minh City, Vietnam. He and his wife have two sons. All the people in his _____ work in Tranh's company. Fourteen other people also work for Tranh. The _____ is in a small building near the city. It makes scissors.

In Vietnam, there was war for many years. Tranh was a soldier in the _____. Some of his workers were also soldiers. Tranh finds old trucks and _____ from the war. His workers take parts to the factory. They make scissors from the parts. They are very good scissors. He sells them in 14 _____ around the world.

Talk to another student. Are your words the same?

Read this story. Think of words for the blanks and write them.

     John Utsi lives in Jokkmokk, Sweden. He is 43 years old. He is a writer for a newspaper. He also writes _____ about the Sami people. In the past, these _____ lived very far from cities. They lived in tents, and they moved the tents often. They went after reindeer. From the reindeer they had milk and _____.

     John's family are Sami people. John and his wife, Elin, and their two daughters live in a city. But every year they go to Lake Kutjaure. They live in a tent for two _____. They go after reindeer. John and Elin work a lot in that time. But they like this life. And the _____ like the tents and the reindeer.

Talk to another student. Are your words the same?

Read the story. Think of words for the blanks and write them.

Salim Al Wahaibi is 12 years old. He lives in Al Mintirib, Oman. Oman is a small country on the Arabian Sea. Salim has a 9-year-old brother, Talib. Five days a week, Salim and Talib _____ to school.

On the weekend, their life changes. Every weekend, there are camel races near Al Mintirib. Salim's father _____ two camels. Salim and Talib get on the camels. Other boys get on other camels. Then all the camels _____ fast. Salim's father _____ a truck next to the camels. He calls to the camels, and he calls to his boys. The other fathers call to their camels and their boys. Then the race _____. But the boys can't stop the camels! The fathers must run and stop them.

Talk to another student. Are your words the same?

Exercise 7

Read the story. Think of words for the blanks and write them.

Leimomi Mapuana lives on the island of Hawaii. She is nine years old. Her parents grow vegetables and fruit. Her father gets _____ from the ocean. They are native Hawaiians. Their families did not _____ to Hawaii from other countries. They lived in Hawaii before Americans or Europeans came to the island.

Leimomi goes to elementary school. But she does not go to the school near her home. Her parents wanted her to learn about the old Hawaii. So she takes a _____ to another school. In some ways, this school is like _____ schools in the United States. The children learn reading, writing, math, science, history, and geography. But in other ways it is very different. In this school, the _____ and teachers speak English only in their English lesson. For their other lessons, they speak Hawaiian. And they _____ about Hawaiian history, music, stories, and dancing.

Talk to another student. Are your words the same?

Read the story. Think of words for the blanks and write them.

Valeriy Korotkov is 45 years old. He lives in the town of Yeniseysk in Russia, but he does not work in Yeniseysk. He works all over Russia. Valeriy's job is not like most jobs. He is a fire fighter. He does not fight fires in _____ or other buildings. He fights forest fires.

He works with a _____ of fire fighters. When there is a forest fire, they get on a plane. The plane flies near the _____ and the fire fighters jump out of the plane. Sometimes it's a big fire and all the trees are burning. Sometimes it's a small fire on the ground. Big or small, the fire fighters try to _____ the fire.

It's a dangerous job, but Valeriy likes it very much. He likes _____ from the planes and he likes working outside. "I could never _____ in an office!" he says.

Talk to another student. Are your words the same?

UNIT 5 Guessing Word Meanings

Context can help you understand new words. You read the context (the sentences) around the new word. Then you make a guess about the meaning.

In these exercises, you can learn to guess from the context. When you are doing the exercises, do not use a dictionary. Do not ask your teacher or your classmates.

After you finish each exercise, you can check the meanings. Then you can use a dictionary or ask your teacher.

Example:

We have a little white cat. She's always hungry. We give her milk in a *bowl* on the kitchen floor. She drinks all the milk in a very short time. Then she wants more!

What is a *bowl*? _It's a large cup._

EXERCISE 1

Write the answers in English or in your own language. Or you can draw a picture.

1. My friend Raymond is a very *lazy* person. He doesn't like to work. He doesn't like to play sports. He likes to sit and watch television. And he likes to sleep.

   What is a *lazy* person? _____

2. Can you see the *nest* in that tree? There are four baby birds in it. They're calling for their mother. Look! Now the mother is coming. She has some food for her babies.

   What is a *nest*? _____

3. My aunt likes to *draw*. She usually draws people or animals, but she also draws trees or flowers. Most of her pictures are in pencil, but sometimes she draws with a pen.

   What does *draw* mean? _____

(continued on next page)

4. I live in a tall building in Chicago. My home is on the sixth floor. But I don't use the *elevator* often. I don't like elevators. They're too small! They're too slow! I like to walk up to the sixth floor.

What is an *elevator*? _____

5. The new store was often empty. This morning there was only one *customer*. She was a young woman. She wanted to buy some Levi's jeans. She didn't like the jeans in the store. So she went away.

What is a *customer*? _____

6. There's a terrible *traffic jam* on the road to London. All the cars are stopped. You can't go left or right. You have to wait for a long time!

What is a *traffic jam*? _____

Talk to another student. Are your answers the same?

EXERCISE 2

Write the answers in English or in your own language. Or you can draw a picture.

1. These bananas are beautiful. But they are not *ripe*. They're still very green. We can't eat them today. Please put them away. We can eat them next week.

What is *ripe* fruit? _____

2. Roger often has *nightmares*. Sometimes they wake him up in the night. He says he sees terrible things in his *nightmares*. Then he can't go back to sleep.

What are *nightmares*? _____

3. There's a *beggar* in front of the store. Poor woman, she doesn't have a coat. It's very cold today. She's asking people for some money. Some people give her money. Other people don't want to look at her.

What is a *beggar*? _____

4. After all the rain, the river is very full. It's full of water and it's full of *trash*. There are old newspapers, boxes, and some chairs. Usually the river is very beautiful, but now it's not beautiful at all.

What is *trash*? _____

5. Bibi is *glad* when it's Friday afternoon. She likes her job, but she likes the weekend more. On Friday afternoon, she takes off her work clothes and puts on her weekend clothes. Then she is ready to have fun.

What does *glad* mean? _____

6. Lily wants to get a *pet*. Her mother says she can't have a dog. Lily asks, "What about a cat?" But Lily's father doesn't want a cat. "What about a bird?" Lily asks. "Okay," say her mother and father. So Lily is going to get a bird.

What is a *pet*? _____

Talk to another student. Are your answers the same?

EXERCISE 3

Write the answers in English or in your own language. Or you can draw a picture.

1. We're going to England for a month. We can go to many cities and towns by train. Then we want to drive to some villages. So we want to *rent* a car. Does it cost a lot in England?

   What does *rent* mean? _____

2. Joe is reading a *poem* by Emily Dickinson. It's a very short poem—25 words. He says it's not easy to read but it is very beautiful and sad.

   What is a *poem*? _____

3. My wife and I want to buy a new car, but we don't have much money. We can't ask my father for help. He doesn't have much money. We have to go to the bank. They can give us a *loan*.

   What is a *loan*? _____

4. Please do not *shout*! My ears are good. I'm here next to you, and I can hear you very well.

   What does *shout* mean? _____

5. There's a terrible *mess* in the kitchen. The sink is full of dirty plates. There's food on the table and paper on the floor. Please clean it all up!

   What is a *mess*? _____

6. Estelle's house was *huge*. It had 25 large rooms. There was also a large and beautiful garden. Some people wanted to buy the house and make a hotel. But Estelle said no. She liked her big house, and she didn't want to move.

   What is a *huge* house? _____

Talk to another student. Are your answers the same?

Write the answers in English or in your own language. Or you can draw a picture.

1. I'm going to the *bakery* now. Do you want some bread? They make very long French bread at the *bakery,* and it's very good. They also make very good cakes and cookies. We often get their chocolate cake.

   What is a *bakery*? _____

2. I'm not going to go to that restaurant again! The food was *awful*! The pizza was black, the vegetables were cold, and the coffee was terrible!

   What is *awful* food? _____

3. The cat has to go to the animal doctor. First, we'll put her in a *cage*. Then we'll put the *cage* in the car. That way she can't run around the car. An angry cat is dangerous in the car.

   What is a *cage*? _____

4. Do you want to go up the mountain? There's only one way. It's up that *path*. It's a small *path* and you can't drive the car on it. You have to park the car here and walk up.

   What is a *path*? _____

5. Please don't *push*! It's too early to go in now. You must all wait and stand in line here. The film doesn't start until 9:00. That's in 20 minutes.

   What does *push* mean? _____

6. Julie is a very *smart* girl. She always has the right answers for the teacher. She does her homework fast. She never has any wrong answers in her homework. Sometimes she helps the other students.

   What is a *smart* girl? _____

Talk to another student. Are your answers the same?

Write the answers in English or in your own language. Or you can draw a picture.

1. Every year there's a big *race* in New York. It's a running *race* for men and women. The people in the *race* have to run 26 miles (42 km). The runners come from many different countries. Many people go to New York to watch the *race*.

   What is a running *race*? _____

2. My friends are getting ready for a party. They have *plenty of* drinks and food, so they don't have to go to the supermarket. They have fruit juice, spring water, coffee, and tea to drink. They have sandwich meat, good bread, chips, beans, and three desserts.

   What does *plenty of* mean? _____

3. My dog likes to play games with me. If I throw a ball far away, he runs after it. He gets it and brings it back. If I throw the ball up, he jumps up. He can *catch* it in the air with his mouth.

   What does *catch* mean? _____

4. I need some help. My car isn't working. This morning the *engine* started and I drove down the street. Then the car stopped. Now I can't start the *engine* again. I think there is something wrong with it.

   What is an *engine*? _____

5. There's a problem with the water on our street. The water company is working on the problem. Their machines are *digging* a big hole under the street. The machines make lots of noise. And the street is a mess!

   What does *digging* mean? _____

6. Kari had a bad *accident* last week. Another car hit his car. The other car was going very fast. It didn't stop at a red light. Kari's car went off the road and hit a wall. Kari had to go to the hospital, but he's okay now.

   What is an *accident*? _____

Talk to another student. Are your answers the same?

Write the answers in English or in your own language. Or you can draw a picture.

1. I'm playing tennis tomorrow with my friend Ombretta. We're playing *against* two women from another town. I don't know these women, but I know they're very good. Sometimes we win our tennis games. I don't think we'll win this time.

   What does *against* mean? _____

2. Next week I'm going to St. Louis. I have to go to a business meeting there. Could you take me to the airport? My *flight* leaves at 10:00, but I need to be there an hour early. I'm flying with American Airlines.

   What is a *flight*? _____

3. Enshi is a very *brave* cat. She's only a little cat, but she's not afraid of big cats. She's not afraid of the big gray cat next door or the big black cat down the street. She fights them all and she sends them away. She doesn't want any other cats in her yard.

   What is a *brave* cat? _____

4. Zoran often *argues* with his father. He's 17 years old and he thinks he is always right. His father thinks he's always wrong. So they *argue* day and night. Zoran's mother doesn't know what to do. She hopes this will stop soon.

   What does *argue* mean? _____

5. Your house has a bad *roof*. You need to do something about it. A new *roof* is expensive. But if you don't get a new *roof*, the rain will come in. Then all your things will get wet. And that will be expensive, too.

   What is a *roof*? _____

6. Last night I had a beautiful *dream*. In the *dream* I was on an island. There was blue water all around the island. The sun was hot, and the water was warm. I went swimming for hours. Then I woke up and it was time to go to work.

   What is a *dream*? _____

Talk to another student. Are your answers the same?

Learning New Words in Categories

In Part 3, Unit 2, you learned new words from your pleasure reading. In this unit, you are going to learn new words in another way—in categories.

A category is like a topic. It tells about words that go together. It helps you remember the words.

Category: Favorite foods in the United States

steak	fried chicken
hamburgers	hot dogs
spaghetti	pizza
tacos	sandwiches
muffins	pancakes
apple pie	ice cream
brownies	chocolate chip cookies

Write the name of your country or home city in the blank. Then write some words for this category.

Category: Favorite foods in _____

_____   _____

_____   _____

_____   _____

_____   _____

Talk to another student about his or her favorite foods.

Think about your favorite place.

Example:

Favorite place: <u>*Yankee Stadium in New York City*</u>

Some words for Yankee Stadium:

baseball	*win*
ticket	*fans*
hot dogs	*radio*
catch	*lights*

Now write your favorite place on the line.

My favorite place: _____

Some words for my favorite place: (You can use a dictionary.)

_____	_____
_____	_____
_____	_____
_____	_____

Show your words to another student. Don't tell your favorite place! Can he or she guess?

Talk about your favorite place. Why do you like it? Use the words on your list.

Do you know all the words on the other student's list? Write the new words in your notebook.

Think about jobs you like. Don't work with another student. Write the names of 10 jobs. Use a dictionary.

Names of jobs

1. _____
2. _____
3. _____
4. _____
5. _____
6. _____
7. _____
8. _____
9. _____
10. _____

Talk to the students in your class. Show your list. Ask each student which job he or she wants. Write a student's name next to every job.

Look at the job list of another student. Do you know all the names of the jobs? Write the new words in your notebook.

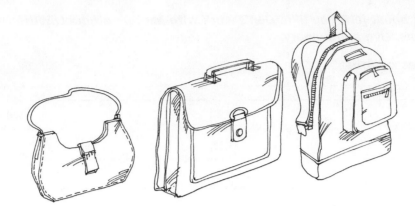

A. Look in your handbag or backpack. Write the names of 10 things you find in it. Use a dictionary. Don't work with another student.

_____   _____

_____   _____

_____   _____

_____   _____

_____   _____

Show your list to another student and look at his or her list. Do you know all his or her words? Write the new words in your notebook.

B. Think of a famous person. Everyone in the class must know this person. It can be a film or music or sports star, a president, a writer, or an artist. What things can we find in that famous person's bag? Write 10 things.

_____   _____

_____   _____

_____   _____

_____   _____

_____   _____

Show your list to another student. Do not tell him or her the name of the person. Can he or she tell you the name?

Look at the other student's list. Who is the person for his or her list? Do you know all his or her words? Write the new words in your notebook.

Which words go with village life? Which words go with city life? Some words can go with both. Write the words under a category. Don't work with another student.

Village Life or City Life?

river	police	newspaper	hole
bicycle	laugh	bridge	afraid
farm	dig	mouse	government
traffic	mountains	doorbell	quiet
apple	park	dirty	noise
fly	cloud	apartment	chicken

Village Life

_____

_____

_____

_____

_____

_____

_____

_____

_____

_____

_____

City Life

_____

_____

_____

_____

_____

_____

_____

_____

_____

_____

_____

Write three more words for village life and three more words for city life.

_____   _____

_____   _____

_____   _____

Look at another student's list. Are your words the same? Write the new words from his or her list in your notebook.

Which things do you like doing? Which things do you not like doing? Write the words under a category. Don't work with another student.

Things I Like Doing and Things I Don't Like Doing

dancing	cooking
restaurants	fishing
walking	sleeping
drinking tea	going to the seaside
playing computer games	listening to music
running	studying English
riding a bicycle	watching television
reading the newspaper	driving a car
working with my hands	going to the movies
buying clothes	writing letters

Things I Like Doing

_____

_____

_____

_____

_____

_____

_____

_____

_____

Things I Don't Like Doing

_____

_____

_____

_____

_____

_____

_____

_____

_____

Look at the lists of the other students in your class. Is any list the same as yours?

Make two categories. Write the categories on the lines. Then write the words under the categories. (Some words can go in both categories.)

office	notebook	manager	pay
lunch	fax	grades	computer
lesson	teacher	telephone	clock
job	erase	classroom	e-mail

Category: _____

Category: _____

_____

_____

_____

_____

_____

_____

_____

_____

_____

_____

_____

_____

_____

_____

_____

_____

Look at another student's categories and lists. Are they the same as yours?

These words are in the stories in Part 1 of this book. Make two categories of words. Then think of names for these categories.

Example:

hungry	easy	wise	terrible	afraid	strong

Category: *bad things*

hungry

terrible

afraid

Category: *good things*

easy

wise

strong

mouse	red	young	old	wolf	big	horse
duck	happy	easy	sheep	strong	turtle	cat

Category: _____

_____

_____

_____

_____

_____

_____

Category: _____

_____

_____

_____

_____

_____

_____

A. Look at the fables and stories in Part 1. Work with another student. Write 20 of the new words you found here.

_____	_____
_____	_____
_____	_____
_____	_____
_____	_____
_____	_____
_____	_____
_____	_____
_____	_____
_____	_____

B. Can you make categories for some of these words? Write the names of the categories and the words.

Category: _____   Category: _____

_____   _____

_____   _____

_____   _____

_____   _____

Category: _____   Category: _____

_____   _____

_____   _____

_____   _____

_____   _____

Work with another pair of students. Do you have the same words and categories?

PART 4

Thinking Skills

Do you think in English when you are reading? Or do you think in your first language? You can understand better if you think in English. These exercises can help you learn to think in English.

Circle the best answer.

Edwin works in a restaurant. He's the only cook. He cooks lunch and dinner. He doesn't cook breakfast. The restaurant is closed

a. in the evening.   c. in the morning.

b. at lunch time.   d. on Tuesdays.

The best answer is c, "in the morning." Morning is the time for breakfast. Edwin doesn't cook breakfast, and Edwin is the only cook. That means the restaurant isn't open for breakfast. So the restaurant is closed in the morning.

Answer a, "in the evening," isn't right. Breakfast isn't an afternoon meal. Dinner is the evening meal, and Edwin cooks dinner. The restaurant isn't closed in the evening.

Answer b, "at lunch time," isn't right. Edwin cooks lunch, so the restaurant isn't closed at lunch time.

Answer d, "on Tuesdays," isn't right. The sentences don't tell about the days of the week.

Guidelines for Thinking Skills Exercises

- Do some thinking skills exercises every week.

- Work quickly and don't use a dictionary.

- Try to guess the meaning of new words.

- Think in English to find the correct answer.

- Remember: Your first guess is often the right one!

Circle the best answer.

1. Can you see that airplane? It's high in the sky. It's going far away. It's going

   a. to school.
   b. home.
   c. to Australia.
   d. to the country.

2. There's a big airplane from Ireland. It's coming down to the airport. Now it's at the airport and all the people are

   a. getting out.
   b. learning English.
   c. sleeping.
   d. buying clothes.

3. When we arrived at the house, there was a big dog in the yard. He was eating his dinner. Then he saw us and looked at us. He was not a nice dog and we were

   a. happy.
   b. afraid.
   c. sad.
   d. hungry.

4. My friend has 15 cats. She has some gray cats and some brown cats. She has a beautiful, young white cat, but she has no

   a. brown cats.
   b. little cats.
   c. brown dogs.
   d. black cats.

5. Juan never drinks tea in the morning. He always drinks coffee. But he often drinks tea in the afternoon. He drinks tea and eats a cake

   a. at 12:00.
   b. at 9:00.
   c. at 3:00.
   d. for breakfast.

EXERCISE 2

Circle the best answer.

1. Surya is in another city for some business meetings. She calls her office every day. Her manager wants to talk with

   a. her.
   b. him.
   c. them.
   d. me.

2. My son's teacher often has meetings. She has meetings with the students and meetings with the other teachers. And she also has meetings with the

   a. men and women.
   b. pencils and paper.
   c. brothers and sisters.
   d. mothers and fathers.

3. Sandra doesn't like her job. She has meetings every week with her manager, and Sandra doesn't like

   a. business.
   b. work.
   c. meetings.
   d. mornings.

4. Chen has a new job in a computer store. A lot of people come to the store. He answers their questions about computers. And he
   - a. sells them books.
   - b. sells them computers.
   - c. buys them computers.
   - d. gives them computers.

5. Bus drivers are often very friendly. They sit in their bus for a long time. They like to talk to the people
   - a. in their car.
   - b. on their bus.
   - c. on the telephone.
   - d. in restaurants.

EXERCISE 3

Circle the best answer.

1. Ron Winston lives in Canada. He likes playing sports a lot. His favorite sports are winter sports. He loves skiing and ice-skating. In fact, Al loves the winter and
   - a. the summer.
   - b. cold weather.
   - c. traveling.
   - d. warm weather.

2. Manuela da Silva is from Portugal. She doesn't like the winter. In winter, the weather is often cold and wet in Portugal. Manuela likes the summer. Her favorite sport is
   - a. windsurfing.
   - b. skiing.
   - c. reading.
   - d. the beach.

3. *The Call of the Wild* is a famous book by Jack London. It tells the story of Buck, a dog. This is a good book for people who love
   - a. mysteries.
   - b. movies.
   - c. telephones.
   - d. animals.

4. There's an important rule in the city. When you cross a street, look both ways. Look to the right and look
   - a. up and down.
   - b. to the left.
   - c. for a policeman.
   - d. at the people.

5. Potatoes are usually very good to eat. But they're not good when they're green. If you find a green potato, you should not eat it. Green potatoes can make you
   - a. sick.
   - b. better.
   - c. well.
   - d. afraid.

Circle the best answer.

1. Selma is from Istanbul. Now she lives in Toronto. She's a writer. She writes books for children. She isn't rich, but she's happy. She likes her work, and she

    a. likes Istanbul.

    b. doesn't like Toronto.

    c. doesn't like Istanbul.

    d. likes Toronto.

2. Virginia lives in a very tall building. Her apartment is on the 40th floor. She likes to look out the windows. At night she can see

    a. cats and dogs.

    b. the sun.

    c. the city lights.

    d. a lot of children.

3. Leo has a very old car. It's 20 years old! It's not very beautiful, and it is not very fast. But it always

    a. goes.

    b. stops.

    c. comes.

    d. sees.

4. A big black cat lives in that house. It sits in the window all day. It likes to look at the people

    a. in the house.

    b. on television.

    c. on the street.

    d. in boats.

5. Tadek almost always has a sandwich for lunch. Sometimes he has an egg sandwich, and sometimes he has a meat sandwich. But today he doesn't want a sandwich for lunch. He wants

    a. some pizza.

    b. breakfast.

    c. a cheese sandwich.

    d. to eat at home.

EXERCISE 5

Circle the best answer.

1. Stella can't find her cell phone. It was in her room yesterday, but today it's not there. She thinks Luis took it, and now she's very

    a. sick with a cold.

    b. ready for class.

    c. happy with Luis.

    d. angry with Luis.

2. Some children are afraid of the dark. They don't like it because they can't see in the dark. At night they always want

    a. the lights on.

    b. the lights off.

    c. the door closed.

    d. the music on.

3. Maria Martinez is 80 years old. She lives in a village near her children and grandchildren. She's very happy now, but she wasn't always happy. When she was young, her life was

    a. easier.   c. better.

    b. difficult.   d. longer.

4. The city of Edinburgh, Scotland, is full of history. It has a beautiful castle, a beautiful church, and many other

    a. interesting old buildings.   c. new movie theatres.

    b. good new restaurants.   d. parks and gardens.

5. Ferrari cars are famous all around the world. People like to look at them in car shows or on television. But most people can't buy them. Ferraris are very

    a. fast.   c. expensive.

    b. beautiful.   d. red.

EXERCISE 6

Circle the best answer.

1. Today, many young women don't know how to cook. They didn't learn from their mothers. Now they buy food that is ready to eat. Or they go

    a. to the supermarket.   c. out to the movies.

    b. out to restaurants.   d. to work early.

2. Michelle and Micol are twin sisters. They look the same, but they are very different. Michelle is very quiet, but Micol likes to talk. Michelle is afraid of new people, but Micol likes

    a. staying alone.   c. meeting new people.

    b. reading books.   d. playing with her sister.

3. Long airplane rides are not fun. You have to stay in your seat for a long time. You can't stand up for long and you can't

    a. sit down.   c. eat any food.

    b. read books.   d. walk around.

4. Peter is 11 years old. He likes running and playing. He doesn't like reading because he doesn't want to

    a. talk to girls.   c. sit still.

    b. go to school.   d. play tennis.

5. In spring, the grass and the trees are green. The flowers are pretty. It's a nice time of year to

    a. visit gardens.   c. go shopping.

    b. study English.   d. play music.

Circle the best answer.

1. The Perez family likes to go to a Cuban restaurant. They go every Saturday evening. They meet their friends at the restaurant, and they have a good

   a. restaurant.

   b. meal.

   c. family.

   d. morning.

2. Dick likes to talk on the telephone. He often talks with his brother in Bombay. He sometimes talks with a friend in Berlin. And every Sunday he talks with his parents in Singapore. Dick pays a lot of money for

   a. clothes.

   b. restaurants.

   c. books.

   d. telephone calls.

3. Laura lived with her mother for most of her life. She never did any housework. Her mother did it all. Then her mother died. At the age of 60, Laura learned to

   a. cook and clean.

   b. read and write.

   c. buy and sell.

   d. work and play.

4. Susan and Sam don't eat French food very often. There is only one French restaurant in their town. The food there isn't very

   a. old.

   b. bad.

   c. open.

   d. good.

5. The life of an artist is not easy. Artists are often very poor because they don't make much money with their art. Many artists are good at making art. But they don't know how to

   a. do it.

   b. sell it.

   c. see it.

   d. buy it.

Circle the best answer.

1. Many people have cell phones. Sometimes they need a cell phone for work. Sometimes they want to talk to friends. Or they want to play games on their phone. There are many good things about cell phones, but there is one bad thing. They are

   a. cheap.

   b. often wrong.

   c. expensive.

   d. easy to use.

2. The Space Needle is a very tall building in Seattle. There's a restaurant at the top. It's not like other restaurants in Seattle. From your table, you can see

   a. all the city.

   b. lots of trees.

   c. a movie.

   d. people eating.

3. Stephen King is a famous American writer. He writes books and stories. Many of his books are also movies. For example, *The Green Mile* is both a book and a

a. story.

b. magazine.

c. television.

d. movie.

4. The first cell phone was made in 1972. It was very big and heavy. Cell phones today are very different. They're

a. very expensive.

b. also very heavy.

c. small and light.

d. made in Finland.

5. In some jobs you have to stand up for many hours. For example, nurses and waiters are always

a. on the telephone.

b. in the room.

c. on a chair.

d. on their feet.

EXERCISE 9

Circle the best answer.

1. Jana often makes chocolate chip cookies. She always brings them when she goes to a party. They're a good party food. Most people like them and they're

a. easy to make.

b. not very good.

c. hard to make.

d. expensive.

2. My cat knows when it's dinner time. She stands in front of the refrigerator. She makes a lot of noise. Then I have to

a. give her some food.

b. drink some milk.

c. wait for her.

d. turn on the light.

3. In Laura's living room there are lots of books and pictures. There are many plants, a piano, and a telephone. But there is no television. Laura doesn't like

a. going swimming.

b. talking on the phone.

c. reading books.

d. watching television.

4. Susanna and Miguel have an ice-cream shop. They work very long hours in the summer. They work less in the spring and fall. In the winter, they close the shop and

a. sell lots of ice cream.

b. make ice cream.

c. work very hard.

d. take a vacation.

5. These days you can do many jobs at home. You need a computer and telephone to work at home. But you don't need a

a. table.

b. car.

c. job.

d. lunch.

Circle the best answer.

1. Tina is in bed. The doctor says she's very sick. She has to take some medicine. She can't get out of bed, and she can't go to

   a. television. c. work.

   b. home. d. children.

2. Donna's father is a doctor. Donna also wants to be a doctor. She wants to be a children's doctor. She likes children, and she wants to help

   a. them. c. students.

   b. animals. d. him.

3. Frank doesn't like to visit hospitals for children. He says they are sad places. In these hospitals there are many sick boys and

   a. doctors. c. mothers.

   b. girls. d. medicines.

4. You can't go to Tom's house today. He's very sick. The doctor is there now. He's looking at Tom, and he is asking Tom's mother a lot of

   a. money. c. questions.

   b. medicine. d. answers.

5. Dr. Kapoor gets up at 6:00 every day and goes to the hospital. In the afternoon, he goes to his office. He gets home at 8:00 in the evening. He has a very long

   a. work. c. office.

   b. time. d. day.

EXERCISE 11

Circle the best answer.

1. Many people have computers at work. Business people have computers in their offices. Teachers have computers at school, and doctors have computers in

   a. rooms. c. hospitals.

   b. restaurants. d. cars.

2. Harold works for a computer company. It's a big company. It has offices in many parts of the world. Harold often travels

   a. for pleasure. c. before lunch.

   b. at home. d. to other countries.

3. Many schools have computers. The children learn about computers in their classes. The teachers use the computers for their

    a. lessons.   c. books.

    b. schools.   d. offices.

4. These shoes are very beautiful, but they're also very expensive. I can't buy them now because I don't have much

    a. money.   c. time.

    b. color.   d. shoes.

5. There are three people in Mohammed's office. They all want to use the computer often, but there's only one computer! Mohammed says they have to get another

    a. car.   c. office.

    b. computer.   d. person.

EXERCISE 12

Circle the best answer.

1. Dan is an English teacher. He works for a big Japanese company. Some people in the company must speak English at work. Dan teaches them

    a. to understand in Japanese.   c. about business.

    b. Japanese.   d. business English.

2. Mara is getting a new pink dress. It's very pretty. Mara is very happy, but her mother is not very happy. The dress is very

    a. pretty.   c. old.

    b. expensive.   d. long.

3. We never go to the French restaurants in New York because they're expensive. We like to go to the Chinese restaurants or the Brazilian restaurants. They

    a. don't cost too much.   c. aren't very good.

    b. cost a lot of money.   d. are hard to find.

4. Tom and Shonni like to go to the Brazilian restaurant because there's often music. Sometimes a Brazilian group plays the music, and the people in the restaurant start dancing. Tom and Shonni

    a. like music and dancing.   c. like Chinese restaurants.

    b. don't like dancing.   d. like Brazilian shoes.

5. Pedro didn't want to get out of bed. He didn't want to have breakfast. He didn't want to go to work. He wanted to

    a. go home.   c. sleep some more.

    b. take the bus.   d. go to school.

Circle the best answer.

1. Anna is a student at the University of Texas. This is her first year. She is studying Spanish. She wants to be a
   a. French teacher.   c. children's doctor.
   b. law student.   d. Spanish teacher.

2. There are many students from other countries at Boston University. Some of these students know English very well, but the other students must
   a. study Chinese.   c. study English.
   b. learn to speak.   d. learn about Boston.

3. I like to go to this store because the people are very friendly. They always smile and say hello. They help you
   a. find things in the store.   c. get a new job.
   b. build a new house.   d. eat your meal.

4. Paula is the new manager of the company. At first, the workers didn't want a woman manager, but now they like her a lot. She's a very friendly person, and she always
   a. walks away.   c. looks at them.
   b. listens to them.   d. talks to women.

5. Suki didn't know any other students at first, but now she knows many of them. She often meets them in the café after class. She says they
   a. always eat ice cream.   c. are always friendly.
   b. usually go home early.   d. never talk to her.

EXERCISE 14

Circle the best answer.

1. Yesterday, the children found a cat. It was very small and young, and it was all alone. The poor thing was very hungry, so we gave it something to
   a. love.   c. do.
   b. fish.   d. eat.

2. Jin often doesn't have time to eat lunch at work. She only has time for coffee. When she comes home from work, she's very hungry. She often
   a. doesn't eat.   c. reads a book.
   b. eats a snack.   d. has no breakfast.

3. Marta could hear the baby crying in the bedroom. It was lunch time, and he was hungry. She turned off the computer. Then she went to the kitchen and got his

    a. bottle.   c. clothes.

    b. breakfast.   d. book.

4. Tommy cries every morning on the way to school because he doesn't want to go to school. He doesn't like the other children, and he doesn't like

    a. his mother.   c. his teacher.

    b. the street.   d. his breakfast.

5. Every night a cat comes into Sam's yard. It cries and cries, and it wakes up Sam. He gets angry and goes out to the yard. But he can never

    a. hear the cat.   c. change the cat.

    b. talk to the cat.   d. find the cat.

EXERCISE 15

Circle the best answer.

1. Raissa's favorite color is blue. She has lots of blue clothes, a blue car, and a blue house. But she doesn't have blue eyes! Her eyes are

    a. big.   c. open.

    b. brown.   d. blue.

2. My parents' favorite restaurant is the Green Garden Restaurant. They like it because it has Chinese food. There is another good restaurant in town, but my mother and father don't go there. It doesn't have

    a. Mexican food.   c. Chinese food.

    b. any food.   d. good food.

3. Daryl doesn't eat lunch at school. She says the food is terrible. There are always hamburgers and pizza, and she prefers to eat

    a. rice and vegetables.   c. terrible food.

    b. school lunches.   d. tea or coffee.

4. Shelley is a terrible student this year. She doesn't go to classes, she doesn't read the course books, and she doesn't do any homework. Her parents are

    a. happy.   c. angry.

    b. hungry.   d. friendly.

5. We don't watch television very often. Our television is very old. We can't hear it very well, and sometimes we can't see it! The picture is in black and white. Soon we'll buy a

    a. bigger television.   c. new television.

    b. new piano.   d. better picture.

Circle the best answer.

1. Bruce Wilson worked for the Acme Paper Company for 40 years. Then last year he stopped working. The people at the company were very sad when he stopped. Bruce was a good worker and

   a. a nice person.   c. a thin person.

   b. an angry person.   d. a young person.

2. There was an interesting movie on television last night. It was the story of an Italian family. The men in the family had lots of problems. In the end, the men all went away. There were only women

   a. on television.   c. in the morning.

   b. in the family.   d. in Italian families.

3. Last year we had a very nice English teacher. She was friendly, and she was a good teacher. This year our English teacher is very different. She's often angry, and she's a

   a. new teacher.   c. tall teacher.

   b. first teacher.   d. terrible teacher.

4. What happened to Juanita yesterday? She wasn't in class. Tanya told me she had some family problems. Do you know about them? I called Juanita's home, but

   a. she was home.   c. there was no answer.

   b. Tanya doesn't know. d. she has no phone.

5. Last week my cat had a big fight with another cat. After that, she stayed away for three days. Then she came back home, but she was

   a. badly hurt.   c. not alive.

   b. very happy.   d. a little cat.

EXERCISE 17

Circle the best answer.

1. Something happened to the computer in the office yesterday morning. It stopped working, and we couldn't start it again. In the afternoon, we did all our work

   a. with the computer.   c. without the computer.

   b. out in the street.   d. on the chalkboard.

2. We went to the hospital this morning. We wanted to see our teacher, but the doctor said no. He said she was still very sick, and he told us to come back

   a. yesterday.   c. to school.

   b. next week.   d. to the hospital.

3. John came to work late again today. He comes late almost every morning! What is the problem? Why is he often late? Doesn't he have a
   a. clock?
   c. bedroom?
   b. bus?
   d. desk?

4. Last year my friend Kiri went to Korea. She wanted to learn about the country and write some newspaper stories. But she had one big problem. She couldn't talk to people because she
   a. didn't like Korean food.
   c. couldn't speak English.
   b. couldn't speak Korean.
   d. didn't have a newspaper.

5. Yesterday we went to see a funny movie. It was a story about love. A man named Jack loved a woman named Jill. Jill loved a man named Jarvis. Jarvis loved a woman named Janet, and Janet loved Jack. All these people had lots of problems, but the movie had
   a. no story.
   c. bad color.
   b. a sad ending.
   d. a happy ending.

EXERCISE 18

Circle the best answer.

1. Many young girls like dancing and go to dance classes. They want to be dancers. They think dancers are beautiful, and they think dancing is fun. But a dancer's life is not always beautiful and fun. They often have
   a. an easy life.
   c. a lot of money.
   b. beautiful legs.
   d. many problems.

2. Saffa was very afraid. There was a mouse in her room. It went under her chair, and then it ran under her bed. She shouted to her mother, "Please come take it away. I don't
   a. like mice!"
   c. see any mice."
   b. eat any animals."
   d. like any animals."

3. Today was a beautiful day. It wasn't very hot, and it wasn't very cold. There was lots of sun, and there wasn't any wind. It was a good day for
   a. walking in the park.
   c. working in the office.
   b. talking on the telephone.
   d. watching television.

4. Last night we went to listen to some music. We didn't have a very nice evening. I almost went to sleep. The music was terrible and the room was
   a. nice.
   c. green.
   b. friendly.
   d. hot.

(continued on next page)

5. The new boy had many problems at school. The other children didn't like him, and the teachers were always angry with him. He told his parents, but they didn't

    a. see him.   c. teach him.

    b. listen to him.   d. wake him.

EXERCISE 19

Circle the best answer.

1. Frank had an important meeting yesterday. He talked to the new manager of the company. The new manager told Frank some good news. He wants Frank to start a new job. It will not be an easy job, but he will

    a. get less money.   c. work long hours.

    b. get more money.   d. have no money.

2. This morning I talked to Mr. Swenson. He told me some interesting news. The town wants to build a new road. They want to build it through his yard. He's very angry and upset. He doesn't want

    a. a road in his yard.   c. any roads in the town.

    b. a new town.   d. to build a road.

3. Yoko was very upset yesterday. Something terrible happened in Japan. There was an earthquake. Many buildings fell down, and about 5,000 people died. Many people now have no homes. They are living in

    a. houses.   c. Japan.

    b. schools.   d. families.

4. Bob's mother is very angry. Bob never wants to do his homework. He also never helps her in the house. Bob is 16 years old. He wants to lie in bed all day and

    a. learn English!   c. listen to music!

    b. work in the kitchen!   d. talk to his parents!

5. There was a dead cat on the road this morning. Leila saw the dead cat and started to cry. Poor Leila. She was very upset. She doesn't like to see

    a. dead animals.   c. lots of cats.

    b. lots of cars.   d. fast cars.

Circle the best answer.

1. Sven was the only child from Sweden. There were some children from Russia, Germany, and England. There were many Italian and Spanish children, but there were no other

    a. American children.

    b. Danish children.

    c. small children.

    d. Swedish children.

2. Dick started a new job last week. He likes the other workers, and he likes the work. There's only one problem. He doesn't like the manager. He says the manager is

    a. always nice.

    b. often angry.

    c. always late.

    d. often hungry.

3. Yussef is not doing very well at the university. He doesn't study for his English class. He only studies for his business class. He says English is not important and he doesn't want to

    a. find it.

    b. feel it.

    c. learn it.

    d. work it.

4. I have some big news for the family! We're going to move to another city next year. The children are going to go to a new school, and I'm going to start a new

    a. job.

    b. day.

    c. car.

    d. family.

5. My cat likes to sit on my car. It's her favorite place. She can see all the people on the street. She can also see all the dogs. The dogs can see her, but they can't

    a. hear her.

    b. catch her.

    c. drive her.

    d. look at her.

Circle the best answer.

1. My brother didn't like playing football or tennis or other sports. He only liked bicycling with his friends. He often went out on his bicycle in the morning and came back in the afternoon. He and his friends went very fast. In a short time they could go
   - a. a few miles.
   - b. another way.
   - c. home.
   - d. many miles.

2. The bus to work is often very slow. There's a lot of traffic in the morning, and the bus has to stop often. When there's traffic, cars are slow, too. But bicycles are not. On a bicycle you can go around and through the traffic. Why don't you go to work by
   - a. bicycle?
   - b. car?
   - c. train?
   - d. bus?

3. Here's your sandwich and some fruit juice. Now take your bicycle and go! You don't want to be late for work. You were late yesterday and the day before. Go fast and
   - a. stop often!
   - b. go home!
   - c. say hello!
   - d. don't stop!

4. Look at all the traffic! We can't get off this road, and we can't go on that road. We have to sit here and wait. The radio doesn't work in this car, so we can't even
   - a. get out of the car.
   - b. listen to any music.
   - c. go home today.
   - d. read the newspaper.

5. Last March I was in Chicago for a business meeting. It's a beautiful city, and I liked it a lot. But I didn't like the weather! It was cold and very, very windy. Now I know why people call Chicago the
   - a. "Sunny City."
   - b. "Windy City."
   - c. "Beautiful City."
   - d. "Business City."

Circle the best answer.

1. Jorge's parents are very interesting people. His mother is a famous eye doctor. His father has a Mexican restaurant in Washington. Many important people eat at his restaurant. One time, the American president

   a. had dinner there.   c. had breakfast in his room.

   b. was in Washington.   d. went to a restaurant.

2. There was a letter on my desk. Now it's not there! Do you know where it is? It's a very important letter. It's from the bank. I have to answer it soon, but I can't

   a. write it.   c. give it.

   b. learn it.   d. find it.

3. Lin lives in New York City. Sometimes she sees famous people near her home. She tells all her friends at work. Her friends live in New Jersey, and they don't often see famous people. Not many famous people

   a. live in New Jersey.   c. live in New York.

   b. go to work.   d. have friends in New York.

4. Some people like to eat too many sweets. Their favorite foods are sweets. They eat lots of ice cream, cake, and cookies. They don't eat much fruit or vegetables. These people are often fat and unhealthy. Sometimes they get very sick. Sweets are not

   a. bad for people.   c. new for people.

   b. good for people.   d. expensive for people.

5. Look at that woman! All the people on the street are looking at her. She's very young and beautiful. She has very nice, expensive clothes. Now some people are taking pictures of her. I think she's famous.

   a. Who are they?   c. Who is she?

   b. What is it?   d. Where are we?

Circle the best answer.

1. Friday was the last day of the English course, and there was a party in the evening. The students bought some food and drinks. They got a stereo and some CDs. Then the party started. The students didn't eat much food. They weren't hungry. They wanted to listen to music and

   a. cook.   c. study.

   b. dance.   d. sleep.

2. Yesterday morning the bank was closed, so I couldn't get any money. I couldn't buy the newspaper, and I couldn't buy any milk or bread. I went to work with no breakfast, and I had nothing to read on the bus. At 11:00 I was very

   a. hungry.   c. rich.

   b. full.   d. tired.

3. Many famous people were at the party in New York City. The president of a big university was there and so was the president of a big company. A famous doctor was there and also a famous writer. There was also

   a. an old friend from school.   c. a large party in New York.

   b. a movie star.   d. a lot of food.

4. Zoe looked at her apartment. It was terrible! There were bottles and glasses on all the tables. There was food on the armchairs and on the floor. She said to her son, "I'm going out for a few minutes. When I come back, I don't want to

   a. see this place!"   c. see these things!"

   b. eat any food!"   d. have a party!"

5. Sonya met a very interesting young man at the party last night. She told me all about him. He's tall and good-looking. He has a very interesting job, and he likes to travel. He's not married, and he doesn't have a girlfriend. I think Sonya is

   a. talking on the telephone.   c. married.

   b. in love with him.   d. going to a party.

Circle the best answer.

1. Did you see the movie on television yesterday evening? It was the true story of Jonah, a young Jewish boy. He lived in Holland in 1941. Then the Germans sent him and his parents to Germany. Jonah lived through this terrible time, but his parents died. It was a very good movie, but very

   a. terrible.   c. happy.
   b. wrong.   d. sad.

2. The English homework for tomorrow is very easy. We have to read one page of our book. We also have to do some exercises in the workbook. I can do it all tomorrow before class. I don't want to do homework this evening. I want to

   a. do my English exercises.   c. speak English.
   b. go out with my friends.   d. do my Spanish homework.

3. The manager at work is angry with me. She says I'm always late. She says I have to be in the office before 9:00 a.m. I can't come at 9:05, and she says I can't go home at 4:50. I can go home only after 5:00 p.m. She says I can't even go out for coffee! I have to drink my coffee

   a. in the office.   c. on the street.
   b. at home.   d. in a restaurant.

4. In 1994, Wanda opened a new store. She sold children's clothing. It was not easy at first, and she had many problems. But after a few years, business was good at the store. Many people in town bought clothes

   a. from friends.   c. in big stores.
   b. at the supermarket.   d. at Wanda's store.

5. Coffee was Ronald's favorite drink. He drank four or five cups of coffee a day. Then the doctor told him to stop drinking coffee. Ronald didn't know what to drink. He didn't want to drink tea. He said, "Only sick people

   a. drink coffee."   c. drink tea."
   b. drink milk."   d. go to the doctor."

Circle the best answer.

1. This is not a good place to live. The weather is terrible. In the summer, it's very hot here. It doesn't rain for three months. In the winter, it's very cold, and it rains all the time. There are only a few nice months

   a. in the year.

   b. for parties.

   c. in Europe.

   d. in the summer.

2. Do you have to go now? You can go home after dinner. I have a very nice meal ready for us. Do you like fish? I have fish and vegetables and rice. I also have cake and ice cream. Please don't go. I can't eat all this food! You must

   a. go home now.

   b. take the train.

   c. help me.

   d. not eat meat.

3. There's no train to our small town, and there are only a few buses. In the morning, people drive their cars to work in the city. In the afternoon, they drive home again. On Saturday and Sunday, the city people drive out here to the country. There is always a lot of traffic

   a. in the city.

   b. in the winter.

   c. on Mondays.

   d. on our roads.

4. Rhonda doesn't like the winter in England. She doesn't like cold weather, and she doesn't like short days. She wants to live in a place with warm winters. She says she's going to sell her house and

   a. build a new one.

   b. start a business.

   c. move to Spain.

   d. go live in Russia.

5. Last summer we went to the mountains for our vacation. We stayed in a beautiful place, and people were very nice to us. But it rained every afternoon! We decided never to go back to the mountains! This summer, we want to go to

   a. the supermarket.

   b. the seaside.

   c. work all summer.

   d. the mountains again.

Teacher's Guide

Introduction

Basic Reading Power is intended for beginning-level students in junior high school, high school, college, or adult education. We assume that students who use this book will have basic decoding skills in English. They will have an English vocabulary of about 300 words, and they will be familiar with the simple present, present continuous, and simple past tenses.

The aim of this book is to teach strategies that will allow students to build on their already-established cognitive abilities and background knowledge. By learning a strategic approach, students will learn to view reading in English as a problem-solving activity rather than a translation exercise. This way, students can learn good reading habits and skills, and they can avoid problems that commonly result from poor reading habits. Students will gain confidence at this early stage, which, in turn, will help them to gain access more quickly to English-language material for study, work, or pleasure.

In *Basic Reading Power,* students are expected to *work on all four parts of the book concurrently* as they develop multiple aspects of their reading ability. This approach is essential for the successful outcome of a reading program using this book. *Basic Reading Power* is intended to prepare students for work in *Reading Power,* which has a similar general approach and layout.

General Guidelines for Teaching Reading with *Basic Reading Power*

- Actively engage students in the reading lesson. It is important for them to enjoy their work and not see the reading lessons as "busywork."
- Have students work in pairs or groups whenever possible. This helps them to develop new thinking styles and increases language acquisition.
- Focus on the thinking processes that the students use to complete the exercises. The right answers are not as important as how the students got those answers.
- Be sure that students know why they are doing an exercise. Awareness of the purpose of their work helps students become involved more actively and results in increased learning.

Part 1: Pleasure Reading

The goal of this part of the book is to introduce students to the idea of extensive reading and to give them the opportunity to experience the rewards of such reading in terms of both improved reading ability and general language ability. To participate successfully in extensive reading, they will need to gain confidence in their abilities and to experience the satisfaction and enjoyment that such reading can bring. For these reasons, teachers should allow students maximum freedom in pacing their reading, choosing their books, and expressing their opinions. Two other factors are also essential for students to discover the pleasure in pleasure reading: a relaxed and trusting atmosphere in the classroom and a high level of enthusiasm and commitment on the part of the teacher.

The extent to which students benefit from their pleasure reading, however, depends on how they go about it. Thus, in this part of the book, students are introduced to some of the ways native speakers approach such reading. These ways include the following:

- reading for the meaning of a story
- predicting what comes next in a story
- responding to the ideas in a story
- relating parts of a story to their own lives
- skipping over unknown words
- breaking a story into parts (analysis)
- talking about a story

The pleasure reading material in the book consists of an introduction, 12 fables, 11 short stories, and 1 long story. It is important that students read these fables and stories in the order presented because the vocabulary and grammatical structures in each story build upon those in previous stories. In the last section of Part 1: Pleasure Reading, students are encouraged to read books for pleasure, and they are guided in the selection of appropriate books.

As mentioned above, the first 12 readings are fables. Since fables are a part of every culture, students will find them easy to relate to. The next 12 stories are about people. They are not fables. You should point out to the students that many of the stories are true or could be true. These stories also provide material for discussion of cultural differences. The main goal for the teacher throughout is to guide the students in learning how to respond to these fables and stories.

Guidelines for Reading the Fables and Stories

General Approach

- Encourage students to talk about each story before, during, and after reading it. As they talk, students make important connections: They connect what they already know and can express in their own language with what they read in the story.

- Lead the discussion at first, in order to model the process for the students. If necessary, provide and practice specific vocabulary for the students to use in such discussions. When the students have had sufficient practice, they should be allowed to lead the discussion themselves.

- Use the first fable ("The Farm Girl and the Milk") as an example with the class. Go through all the reading steps together with them.

Before Reading a Fable or Story

- Encourage students to preview the story. Tell them to look at the title and at any illustrations accompanying the story and to identify what they see.

- Lead students to make predictions about the story by asking them the following questions. Be sure to have them explain their answers as well.

  What is the story about?

  Who are the people in the story?

  Where are they?

  Is this story about today or about the past?

  Do you think it is a sad story or a happy one?

  Do you think the story is true?

- Ask students to read the first paragraph of the story. Then have them make more predictions about what comes next.

Reading the Fable or Story

- Ask students to read the story silently all the way through. Tell them not to stop and look up unfamiliar words in the dictionary. Instead, instruct them to put a checkmark with a pencil next to the words they don't know. Then they should continue reading.

- Tell the students that they will have an opportunity to look up the new words later on.

After Reading the Fable or Story

- Put students in small groups and ask them to retell the story to each other.

- Then lead the whole class in reconstructing the story together. Discuss with students their responses to the story by asking them questions such as these:

  Did you like this story? Why or why not?

  Who is in the story?

  Do you think it is a true story?

How did the story make you feel?

Is the ending a good one?

How could we change the ending?

- Ask students to read the story again silently. If an illustration accompanies the story, tell them to label parts of it with names and words from the story.

- Ask students to look back at the story and underline any words that are still unfamiliar to them. They should write those words on the lines below the story or in a personal vocabulary notebook and look up the meanings in their dictionaries. They may need help in finding the correct meaning and in wording a satisfactory definition. Show the students how this is done and assist students in learning to use the dictionary independently.

Additional Activity

As a whole-class activity after reading the story, ask students to form small groups and brainstorm about other possible endings. Working with the whole class, ask students to dictate the best ending they have come up with. Write that ending on the board and then ask students to copy it into their notebooks. After some practice, individual students can try to write their own endings and then compare their endings with those of other students. Have students write another ending as a homework assignment.

Pleasure Reading Books

Evaluating Students' Progress

There are a number of ways you can evaluate students' progress and comprehension in their pleasure reading books. Whatever method you choose, however, you must keep the "pleasure" in mind. Therefore, feedback to students should be positive and should focus on their personal reactions to their reading. In addition, students' output, whether oral or written, should not be judged on pronunciation or grammar.

Here are some ways to evaluate pleasure reading:

- Individual teacher/student conferences. This is the best way for you to come to a quick assessment of each student's understanding of what he or she is reading. These conferences can give the student an opportunity for a one-to-one discussion with you in which you can model ways that native speakers talk about literature. The focus of these talks should be the student's response to the book, rather than a retelling of the story. By giving individual attention to students, these conferences can also help students build confidence in their abilities. Avoid asking individual students to stand up and report orally on the reading in front of the whole class, which could be damaging to students' self-confidence.

- Pleasure Reading Book List. (See text, page 41.) Keep track of the number of books read by referring to this list. As a variation, keep book lists for each student posted in the classroom. With younger or competitive students, this tactic can be motivating, though care must be taken to keep the competitive aspect from becoming too serious.

- Writing about Pleasure Reading Books. (See text, pages 40-41). This letter-writing activity encourages students to put down on paper their thoughts about a book in an informal context. The letters can be written in class or assigned as homework. Then students can exchange letters, or you can select some letters to read aloud or write on the board. Other students who have read the same book can be asked their opinions. The emphasis of any discussion should, as always, be on the students' reactions, not on details of the story.

- Pleasure Reading Report. (See text, page 40.) Though long, formal book reports are not recommended, a short report following a simple format can be filled in by the student on completion of each book and kept on file in the class or in the student's notebook. They can then be read aloud and compared if more than one student has read a particular book. In addition, if the reports are kept on file in the classroom, students can refer to them in choosing books.

Choosing Books for Pleasure Reading

Students' limited vocabulary does not necessarily mean a limited choice of reading material for them. Many publishing companies produce books for the beginning, or "starter," level, with a wide range of subject matter to interest both younger and more mature students.

Many teachers have found that the question of how to provide pleasure reading for all their students can best be resolved by starting a class lending library with a few more titles than there are students, so that each student will be able to choose a book. It may also be possible to combine libraries with another teacher or teachers or to set up the pleasure reading collection in the school library. In this case, however, students need to have free and frequent access to the library.

Aside from being able to choose subject matter that is interesting to them, students also need to be free to choose books at an appropriate level. Be sure to include books at a somewhat higher level for those students who quickly gain confidence and want more challenging reading, as well as very easy books for those students who progress more slowly.

The following list contains a few of the many titles available.

Very Low Level

Longman

Longman Easystarts—200-word vocabulary. These books are all 16 pages long and come with a cassette recording of the text. Examples:

April in Moscow	Stephen Rabley
Between Two Worlds	Stephen Rabley
Dead Man's River	Elizabeth Laird
Dino's Day in London	Stephen Rabley
Who Wants to Be a Star?	Margaret Iggulden

Longman Originals—Stage 1: 300-word vocabulary. Cassettes available. Examples:

Ali and His Camera	Raymond Pizante
Marcel and the Shakespeare Letters	Stephen Rabley
Mike's Lucky Day	Leslie Dunkling
The Missing Coins	John Escott
The Wrong Man	Kris Anderson

Longman Structural Readers—Stage 1: 300-word vocabulary. Cassettes available. Examples:

Aladdin and His Magic Lamp	A. Stempleski
Car Thieves	L. G. Alexander

The Flying Spy	Alwyn Cox
Green Island	A. G. Eyre
Kate and the Clock	Leslie Dunkling
The Mystery of the Loch Ness Monster	Leslie Dunkling

Heinemann Educational Books, Inc.

Heinemann ESL Guided Readers—Starter Level: 300-word vocabulary. Examples:

Alissa	*The Lost Ship*
Blue Fins	*Sara Says No!*
The Briefcase	*Ski Race*
L.A. Detective	

More Advanced Level

Oxford University Press

Oxford Bookworms—Level 1: 400-word vocabulary. Examples:

The Coldest Place on Earth	*The President's Murderer*
The Elephant Man	*Under the Moon*
Love or Money	*White Death*

Longman

Longman Structural Readers—Stage 2: 500-word vocabulary. Examples:

Adventure Story	L. G. Alexander
The Boy and the Donkey	Celia Turvey
Girl Against the Jungle	Monica Vincent
Have You Got Our Ticket?	Ian Serraillier
Shakespeare Detective and Other Short Stories	S. H. Burton

Longman Classics—Stage 1: 500-word vocabulary. Examples:

Alice in Wonderland	Lewis Carroll
Black Beauty	Anna Sewell
Heidi	Johanna Spyri
The Three Musketeers	Alexandre Dumas

Longman Originals—Stage 2: 600-word vocabulary. Cassettes available. Examples:

Another World	Elaine O'Reilly
Fire in the Forest	Ian Swindale
Wanted: Anna Marker	Kris Anderson

Part 2: Comprehension Skills

General Guidelines

- You should always make sure that the students understand the purpose of the exercises they are doing and how the particular skill relates to general reading ability. Otherwise, the exercises become busywork and the students lose interest.

- The whole class should work together when the teacher introduces and works on the first exercise in a unit.

- You should model the thinking processes that students need to use to carry out the exercise. That is, you should "think out loud" in front of the class so that students can learn about those processes and the language used to talk about them.

- It is best to have the students work in pairs or small groups whenever possible.

- Since the exercises in each unit become gradually more difficult, students should always work on them in the order in which they are presented.

- The exercises in this part of the text should be approached as much as possible in a spirit of playful competition. When the exercises are treated like games and the atmosphere of the class is relaxed, students become more involved and feel freer to take risks.

- For some of the exercises, students may give answers that are different from those in the Answer Key, and any reasonable answers should be accepted as long as the student can justify them.

Unit 1: Scanning for Key Words

The scanning exercises in Units 1 and 2 are designed to help students get over the habit of reading every word on a page. In scanning, students must quickly look for specific information, skipping over unneeded words. In this unit, students scan across a line for a key word. Note that the words used in the exercises are from the list of the "100 Words" in Part 3, Unit 3. In doing these exercises, students will also be working to improve their sight recognition of these important words—the 100 most common words in English. (You can refer to page 191 in this Teacher's Guide for more information about the 100 words.)

Since speed is essential for scanning, encourage students to work quickly, either by timing them or by conducting the exercises as a kind of race among pairs of students.

Unit 2: Scanning for Information

In these exercises, students scan a variety of real-life materials for the answers to some specific questions. In doing this, they will learn to move their eyes quickly across a page and not be distracted from their search for information. Again, speed is important. The material in this unit can also serve as a source for discussion of certain aspects of U.S. culture and how they compare with other cultures.

In each exercise in Unit 2, students have opportunities to interact with other students. In part B, students are asked to form questions and ask another student to scan for the answers. In part C, they are asked to discuss the content of the exercise with another student.

Note that students should not use a dictionary while working on the scanning exercises but should skip any words they do not know. Discuss some of the vocabulary afterwards in a general discussion about the material.

Unit 3: Making Inferences

Students should be taught that good readers often have to "read between the lines" in order to get the meaning of a passage. To do this, students must be willing to make guesses—which means taking risks. These exercises will help them gain confidence in their ability to infer meaning in a reading text.

In each exercise, students are asked to work with another student or to compare their answers after doing the exercise. These activities are essential; in talking about their inferences, students can increase their ability to justify their answers and to ask and answer clarification questions. Explaining their thinking is very important for improving reading.

In this unit, getting the "right answer" is less important than the thinking process that students go through to get their answers. Allow students the opportunity to come up with different answers if they can justify their ideas based on information in the passage.

As in other units, students often enjoy a class discussion of the materials in Unit 3, after the exercises have been completed.

Unit 4: Understanding Sentences

The ability to find meaning in a sentence is a skill that good readers in English frequently take for granted.

Students at this low level need practice in reading sentences carefully. This can be accomplished by working on forming good sentences and identifying the parts of the sentences most important to the meaning. Though this is not always thought of as a reading skill, it is important to remember that the thinking processes involved in reading and writing are often inseparable.

In these exercises, students will have the opportunity to be creative in forming sentences. However, their sentences must always be grammatically correct and reflect correct usage. Note that in Exercises 1 through 7, there are several possible ways to connect the parts of the sentences but only a few ways that they can be connected into correct sentences using each part only once.

Unit 5: Looking for Topics

In English texts, ideas are generally expressed and developed in a "topic-centered" way; that is, writers first give the topic and then they comment on it. In learning to read fluently in English, it is essential that students begin early on to think in terms of the topic.

These exercises work best if the students work in pairs. That way, the two students can help each other when one or the other does not understand. Furthermore, in talking to each other about the topic, the students will develop their metacognitive ability to think and speak about a text in terms that will help them to comprehend what they read.

A further reason for working in pairs is that if one of the pair of students does not know a particular word in an exercise, there is a good chance that their partner will. This means students will be able to avoid using the dictionary when working on the topics exercises.

Unit 6: Comprehending Paragraphs

This unit aims to provide the students with more practice in recognizing the topic-centered nature of English texts. Students must first understand that good comprehension depends on the reader's ability to identify the topic. Good readers, in fact, are always unconsciously or consciously looking for the topic as they read.

Students then need to understand how a paragraph in a text focuses on a topic. For that reason, the purpose of the first two exercises is to familiarize students with the difference between a paragraph and a random group of sentences.

Students who need more practice in recognizing the form of a paragraph can be given this further assignment: Tell students to choose one of the groups of sentences about New York (Exercise 1—paragraphs 1, 3, and 4) or Music (Exercise 2—paragraphs 1, 4, and 5) that makes a good paragraph and write the paragraph in their notebook. Remind them to begin the paragraph by indenting the first sentence.

As they write out the paragraph, students will have an opportunity to notice again that every sentence in the paragraph refers to the same topic. Often beginning-level students need this kind of reinforcement in order to internalize both the form and the topic-centered nature of a paragraph in English.

Exercises 3 and 4 give students another opportunity to write out sentences in paragraph form. Exercises 5 through 8 give students practice first in recognizing the topic and then in thinking of the topic and stating it in comprehensible form. Where students are asked to think of the topic, various answers are, of course, acceptable, as long as they express the topic correctly (neither too specific nor too general).

Exercises 9 and 10 are more challenging. They require students to discriminate between sentences that fit and do not fit in a specific paragraph. Exercises 11 and 12 give students further practice in constructing paragraphs.

As in all the other skills units, allow time for discussion about how students came up with their answers. Encourage students to talk explicitly about the thinking processes involved.

Teachers who are looking for further work on topics of paragraphs will find a more extensive treatment (at a high-beginner level) in *Reading Power*.

Part 3: Vocabulary Building

Research in second-language reading confirms what many teachers know by instinct and experience: Building vocabulary is an essential factor in reading improvement, especially at the lower levels.

In this part of the book, students are encouraged to build vocabulary in various ways. Some of the exercises are meant to give students an opportunity to learn words that are most often found in texts in English. Other exercises give students practice in recognizing

word structures. Many of the exercises present unfamiliar words in meaningful contexts so that students can learn to use such contexts to figure out meaning through the application of cognitive skills. In fact, the more cognitive capacity required in the process of figuring out meaning, the more likely students are to fix the word and the meaning in their long-term memory.

For this reason, in completing Units 4 and 5, students should be discouraged from using their dictionaries or asking friends or teachers for the meanings. Instead, encourage them to try to establish meaning first by thinking about the context and making guesses. Only then should the dictionary come into play, as a means to check the guesses. This approach is established from the very beginning, in Part 1 of the book, where students are asked not to use dictionaries while reading for pleasure.

Unit 1: Noticing Word Parts

Recent research has shown that the decoding skills (the ability to process the letters on the page) are slower to develop than was previously believed. Practice in word segmentation, as in these exercises, is a key step in developing decoding skills. Research has also shown that English-language learners often try to process English words the same way that they process words in their first language. However, the process is different from language to language and the ability of students to decode in English may be hindered by what they have learned in their native language, especially if that language has a different alphabet or no alphabet. By raising students' consciousness of spelling patterns in English, these exercises will allow them to develop new ways of processing words in English.

While the exercises here may appear similar to the scanning exercises in Part 2, the aim is very different and so these should **not** be timed. Students should be able to take their time in completing the exercises so that they can focus on the spelling patterns.

It is important to keep in mind that these are not meant to be exercises in pronunciation. They are meant to help students notice how words are put together. While students should not be asked to produce the sounds of these words, because that involves a whole different set of skills, they can learn to recognize sounds. To this end, it can be helpful for students to hear the words as they are reading them. The teacher can read the words aloud as they do these exercises. Research suggests that the ability to hear the different sounds and to match the sounds with their spelling does reinforce decoding skills in reading.

Unit 2: New Words from Your Reading

This unit should be introduced after students have read several of the fables in Part 1: Pleasure Reading. Below each fable, students will have written some new words. They should then choose 10 of these words to transcribe onto the pages of this unit.

These words may, of course, be different for different students, thus allowing them to develop their own personal vocabulary learning project. Having learned the procedure for writing the new word, the sentence or sentences, and the meaning, students should then continue this practice in their own notebooks. Ideally, these should be small notebooks that they can easily carry around and that are used exclusively for this purpose.

At the end of a week or other given period of time, have students test their knowledge of the new words of that week by giving themselves a New Words Quiz (see page 126). Verify that students quiz themselves in this way at regular intervals throughout the course.

Unit 3: The 100 Words

In this unit, students are asked to focus their attention on the 100 most common words in English. Although these words are often taken for granted by teachers, they are not always easily learned through context, and they often constitute a serious stumbling block for the beginning reader. Be aware, in fact, that these 100 most common words make up 50 percent of the words in an English text of average difficulty! If students have to stop and think about these words, their reading speed and comprehension will obviously suffer.

Therefore, it is essential that students learn to recognize these common words on sight. That is the aim of this unit and the reason students are asked to concentrate on the spelling and form of each word, rather than the grammar or meaning.

Unit 4: Learning about Context

In this unit, students are introduced to the concept of context in vocabulary learning. Emphasize the relationship of the word to the general context of the story or the more specific context of the sentence, and ask students to be explicit about the reasons for their choice of words. In Exercises 1 through 4, the missing words are given to the students, but in the later exercises, students must think of the missing words. They may come up with some different answers from those suggested in the Answer Key; these should be accepted as long as they make sense.

Unit 5: Guessing Word Meanings

In this unit, students are now faced with words that are probably unfamiliar to them. In order to arrive at some kind of meaning for the words, they must tap their own experience and knowledge of the world. Note that students should ideally try to write definitions in English, however vague or circuitous they may be, as this is excellent practice. However, if that is not possible due to the level of proficiency or maturity of the class, they may write equivalent words in their own language.

You should go through the first exercise with the whole class as a group and model the thought processes that help the reader use the contextual clues to arrive at a hypothetical meaning. Afterwards, have students try to do several items on their own and then work in pairs to compare their answers or figure out together meanings they haven't deciphered individually. If you are working with students whose language is unfamiliar to you, students should do this pair work with another student who speaks the same language, especially if students cannot think of the word in English but can think of an equivalent word in their own language.

Unit 6: Learning New Words in Categories

This unit builds on the use of students' own life experiences to help them learn new words in categories. Grouping the words in categories puts them into context for the students and so increases the probability of retention. Furthermore, the personal involvement required in the exercises is a further positive influence on the acquisition and retention of the vocabulary. Therefore, these exercises require a large degree of individual input on the part of the students and allow them to choose the vocabulary to be learned to a large extent.

In Exercise 1, explain the example. Then, using your own favorite place, do another example on the chalkboard with the group.

This will make clear to them how to do their own favorite place.

In Exercises 4–8, encourage students to create categories that reflect their own life experience, and after each exercise ask them to explain their categories to the class. For example, in Exercise 4, one student might put "mountains" in "Village Life" (e.g., a Swiss village) and another student might put "mountains" under "City Life" (e.g., Mexico City).

Part Four: Thinking Skills

These exercises provide practice in some of the basic thought patterns of English. Students can solve the problems presented in the exercises by applying such patterns as synonymy, opposites, analogies, negation, part–whole relationships, and drawing conclusions based on evidence.

The exercises gradually become more difficult, so it is important that they be assigned in the order they are presented in the book. Once again, the use of dictionaries should be discouraged while students work on the thinking skills exercises.

In this part of the book, students should work alone. Once all students have completed a set of problems, either in class time or as a homework assignment, check them together in a group session in which students volunteer to read the items aloud. Encourage students to express their disagreement if they have different answers and ask them to explain how they arrived at those answers. This kind of discussion can help them externalize their thinking processes and lead them to greater metacognitive awareness.

Sample Syllabus

Basic Reading Power	Part 1 Pleasure Reading	Part 2 Comprehension Skills	Part 3 Vocabulary Building	Part 4 Thinking Skills
Week 1	• Read Teacher's Guide, pp. 183–187. • Introduce book, p. v. • Work on pp. vi–vii. • Introduce Part 1, pp. 1–41. • Introduce Unit 1, Fables, p. 4. • Do Fable 1, p. 4. Make sure students apply the four steps listed on p. 3 "Reading to Understand Stories." • Do Fable 2, p. 6.	• Read Teacher's Guide, pp. 188–190. • Introduce Part 2, Unit 1, Scanning for Key Words, p. 43. • Make sure that students understand that scanning is a very fast kind of reading. • Do Exercises 1, 2, 3, 4, & 5, pp. 43–46.		
HOMEWORK	Fable 3, p. 7.	No Scanning for homework		
Week 2	• Talk about Fable 3 and make sure students write new words in Step 4. • Do Fables 4 & 5, pp. 8–10. Make sure students carry out all four steps, especially Step 3, "Talk about the story." and Step 4, "Write new words."	• Do Scanning Exs. 6, 7, 8, 9 & 10, pp. 47–51. • Introduce Unit 2, Scanning for Information, p. 52. • Do Exercises 1, 2, & 3, pp. 52–57. In each exercise, teach students to form questions for Part B. Discuss Part C in pairs.	• Read Teacher's Guide, pp. 190–192. • Introduce Part 3, Unit 1, Noticing Word Parts, p. 116. • Explain p. 116, do example. • Do Exercises 1, 2, & 3, pp. 116–118. These are not timed exercises.	
HOMEWORK	Fable 6, pp. 11–12. Write down new words in Step 4.	No Scanning for homework.	Exs. 4, 5, & 6, pp. 118–119.	

Sample Syllabus

	Part 1 **Pleasure Reading**	Part 2 **Comprehension Skills**	Part 3 **Vocabulary Building**	Part 4 **Thinking Skills**
Week 3	• Talk about Fable 6. • Do Fables 7 & 8, pp. 12–14. Make sure students carry out all 4 steps.	• Do Exs. 4, 5, & 6, pp. 15–18. Be sure students always do the work very quickly. • Introduce Unit 3, Making Inferences. Discuss example, p. 64. • Do Exs. 1, 2, 3, & 4, pp. 65–69. Students should work in pairs and discuss their work.	• Check homework. • Do Ex. 7, pp. 120–121. • Introduce Unit 2, New Words from Your Reading, p. 122. • Instruct students to write some new words from the Fables on pp. 122–124.	• Read Teacher's Guide, p. 192. • Introduce Part 4, p. 163. • Do Ex. 1, p. 164. • Students should work alone and without a dictionary. Afterwards, ask volunteers to read the items aloud. Encourage discussion when students' answers vary.
HOMEWORK	Read Fable 9, pp. 14–15.	Inference Exercises 5 & 6, pp. 70–71.	Unit 1, Ex. 8, p. 121. Instruct students to bring in a small, pocket-sized notebook.	Exs. 2 & 3, pp. 164–165.
Week 4	• Talk about Fable 9. • Do Fable 10, p. 16. • Review the four steps.	• Check homework. • Do Exs. 7 & 8, pp. 72–73. • Encourage students to talk to each other about their work.	• Check homework. • Write new words from Step 4 of Fables. • Write in more words on pp. 122–124. • Start a vocabulary notebook as instructed on p. 124. • Explain the New Words Quiz.	Check homework on Exs. 2 & 3. Ask volunteers to read the items aloud. Encourage discussion when answers vary.
HOMEWORK	Fable 11, pp. 17–18. Write new words in vocabulary notebook.	Ex. 9, p. 74.	Find new words for notebook.	Exs. 4 & 5, p. 166.
Week 5	Talk about Fable 11. Make sure students follow the four steps. Ask students to share their new words with the class.	• Check homework. • Do Ex. 10, p. 75 • Introduce Unit 4, Understanding Sentences. • Do Exs. 1, & 2, pp. 76–77.	• Introduce Unit 3, The 100 Words, p. 129. Read the words aloud to the students. • Do Exs. 1, 2, 3, & 4, pp. 130–131.	Check homework on Exs. 4 & 5. Ask volunteers to read the items aloud. Encourage discussion when answers vary.
HOMEWORK	Read Fable 12, pp. 18–19. Write new words in vocabulary notebook.	Ex. 3, p. 78.	Exs. 5, 6, & 7, pp. 132–134.	Exs. 6 & 7, pp. 167–168.

	Part 1 Pleasure Reading	Part 2 Comprehension Skills	Part 3 Vocabulary Building	Part 4 Thinking Skills
Week 6	• Talk about Fable 12. • Introduce Unit 2, Stories, p. 20. Do Story 1 & Story 2. Make sure students follow the four steps	• Check homework. • Do Exs. 4 & 5, pp. 79–80.	• Check homework. • Do Exs. 8, 9, & 10, pp. 135–139. • Introduce Unit 4, Learning about Context, p. 140. • Talk about the example, p. 140. • Do Ex. 1, pp. 140–141. Students should work alone. Encourage class discussion after work is completed.	Check homework on Exs. 6 & 7. Ask volunteers to read the items aloud. Encourage discussion when answers vary.
HOMEWORK	Read Story 3, p. 23. Write new words in vocabulary notebook.	Exs. 6 & 7, pp. 81–82.	Exs. 2, 3, & 4, pp. 141–143.	Exs. 8 & 9, pp. 168–169.
Week 7	• Talk about Story 3. Did students do all four steps? • Do Stories 4 & 5, pp. 24–25. Make sure students follow the four steps.	• Check homework. • Do Exs. 8, 9 & 10, pp. 82–85. Students should work in pairs.	• Check homework. • Do Exs. 5 & 6, pp. 144–145. • Encourage class discussion. • Prepare students for a vocabulary quiz on their individual new word lists.	Check homework on Exs. 8 & 9. Ask volunteers to read the items aloud. Encourage discussion when answers vary.
HOMEWORK	Read Story 6, pp. 26–27. Write new words in vocabulary notebook.	Exs. 11 & 12, p. 86 .	Exs. 7 & 8, pp. 145–146. Prepare for vocabulary quiz.	Exs. 10 & 11, pp. 170–171.
Week 8	• Talk about Story 6. Ask students to share their new words with the class. • Do Story 7 and Story 8, pp. 27–29. Make sure students follow the four steps.	• Check homework. • Introduce Unit 5, Looking for Topics, "Topics That Are Names of Groups," p. 87. • Do Exs. 1 & 2, pp. 87–89	• Check homework. • Vocabulary quiz. • Introduce Unit 5, Guessing Word Meanings, p. 147. • Talk about intro., p. 147. • Do Exs. 1 & 2, pp. 147–149.	Check homework on Exs. 10 & 11. Ask volunteers to read the items aloud. Encourage discussion when answers vary.
HOMEWORK	Read Story 9, pp. 29–30. Write new words in vocabulary notebook.	Ex. 3 p. 90.	Exs. 3 & 4, pp. 149–150.	Exs. 12 & 13, pp. 171–172.

	Part 1 Pleasure Reading	Part 2 Comprehension Skills	Part 3 Vocabulary Building	Part 4 Thinking Skills
Week 9	• Talk about Story 9. Ask students to share their new words with the class. • Do Story 10 and Story 11, pp. 30–32. Make sure students follow the four steps.	• Check homework. • Introduce "Topics That Name Things with Many Parts," p. 91. • Do Exs. 4–5, pp. 91–92. • Do Ex. 6, p. 93. • Notice that in Exs. 6–12, students can find both kinds of topics.	• Check homework. • Do Exs. 5 & 6, pp. 151–152. • Check students' vocabulary notebooks.	Check homework on Exs. 12 & 13. Ask volunteers to read the items aloud. Encourage discussion when answers vary.
HOMEWORK	Read Story 12, pp. 32–36. Write new words in vocabulary notebook.	Topics Exs. 7, 8 & 9, pp. 94–96.	Ex. 4, p. 150.	Exs. 14 & 15, pp. 172–173.
Week 10	• Talk about Story 12. • Introduce Unit 3, Reading Books for Pleasure, p. 37. Students should understand that pleasure reading is very important for learning English. • Help students select pleasure reading books. Each student should read a different book. • Have students write information about their books on the Pleasure Reading Book List, p. 41.	• Check homework. • Do Exs. 10, 11, & 12, pp. 97–99. • Introduce Unit 6, Comprehending Paragraphs. Discuss examples, p. 100. • Do Ex. 1, pp. 101–102.	• Check homework. • Introduce Unit 6, Learning New Words in Categories, p. 153. Explain example. • Students should talk about their words. • Do Ex. 1, p. 154. • Check students' vocabulary notebooks.	Check homework on Exs. 14 & 15. Ask volunteers to read the items aloud. Encourage discussion when answers vary.
HOMEWORK	Pleasure reading 30 min./day. Write new words in notebook.	Ex. 2, pp. 102–103.	Ex. 2, p. 155.	Exs. 16 & 17, pp. 174–175.

	Part 1 Pleasure Reading	Part 2 Comprehension Skills	Part 3 Vocabulary Building	Part 4 Thinking Skills
Week 11	• Check students' progress in their pleasure reading books. • Ask each student to tell the class the title of their book and how many pages they have read. • Introduce "Talking about Pleasure Reading Books," p. 38. Check students' progress in their pleasure reading books.	• Check homework. • Do Exs. 3 & 4, pp. 103–104. • Discuss the example in Ex. 5, pp. 104–105. Then complete Ex. 5, pp. 105–106. • Students should work together.	• Check homework. • Do Ex. 3, p. 156. • Check students' vocabulary notebooks. Check the accuracy of their definitions.	Check homework on Exs. 16 & 17. Ask volunteers to read the items aloud. Encourage discussion when answers vary.
HOMEWORK	Pleasure reading 30 min./day. Write new words in vocabulary notebook.	Ex. 6, pp. 106–107.	Ex. 4, p. 157. Prepare for a vocabulary quiz on individual new words in notebooks.	Exs. 18 & 19, pp. 175–176.
Week 12	• Check students' progress in their pleasure reading books. • Introduce "Writing about Pleasure Reading Books," pp. 39–40.	• Check homework. • Do Exs. 7 & 8, pp. 107–108.	• Check homework. • Check students' vocabulary notebooks. Make sure that the definitions that they wrote are accurate. • Do Exs. 5 & 6, pp. 158–159.	Check homework on Exs. 18 & 19. Ask volunteers to read the items aloud. Encourage discussion when answers vary.
HOMEWORK	Pleasure reading 30 min./day. Write new words in vocabulary notebook.	Ex. 9, pp. 109–110.	Exs. 7 & 8, pp. 160–161. Prepare for a vocabulary quiz on individual new words in notebooks.	Exs. 20 & 21, pp. 177–178.

Sample Syllabus

	Part 1 Pleasure Reading	Part 2 Comprehension Skills	Part 3 Vocabulary Building	Part 4 Thinking Skills
Week 13	When students finish reading a book, they should write a letter to a friend or a report, as on p. 40.	• Check homework. • Do Ex. 10, pp. 110–111.	• Check homework. • Help students prepare for vocabulary quiz. • Give vocabulary quiz on words from vocabulary notebooks.	Check homework on Exs. 20 & 21. Ask volunteers to read the items aloud. Encourage discussion when answers vary.
HOMEWORK	Pleasure reading 30 min./day. Write new words in vocabulary notebook.	Ex. 11, pp. 112–113.	Each student should prepare to teach one new word to the class.	Exs. 22 & 23, pp. 179–180.
Week 14	Each student should tell the class about their book.	• Check homework. • Do Ex. 12, p. 114.	Each student should teach one new word to the class.	• Check homework. • Do Exs. 24 & 25, pp. 181–182, as a final quiz on Thinking Skills. • Talk about progress in learning to think in English.

Credits

Text credits

Page 37, excerpt from *Simon and the Spy,* by Elizabeth Laird. © 1995 by Addison Wesley Longman; **Page 40,** based on an idea from Charlotte Seeley, **Page 72,** excerpt from *Dead Man's River* by Elizabeth Laird. © 1990 by Addison Wesley Longman; **Page 73,** excerpt from *Tinker's Farm* by Steven Rabley. © 1990 by Addison Wesley Longman; **Page 72,** excerpt from *Island for Sale* by Anne Collins. © 1992 by Addison Wesley Longman. All reprinted by permission of Addison Wesley Longman Ltd; **Page 75,** excerpt from *Brown Eyes* by Paul Stewart. © 1991 by Penguin Longman Readers; **Page 63** table of contents from *Making Business Decisions,* by Frances Boyd. © 1994 by Addison Wesley Longman. Reprinted by permission of Addison Wesley Longman.

Text art/Photos

Pages vii, 13, 14, Dalsy de Puthod; **Pages 4, 6, 11, 17, 20, 84, 87–91, 101, 140–146, 156,** Bill Peterson; **Pages 37–38,** David Simonds, from *Simon and the Spy,* © 1995 by Addison Wesley Longman Ltd; **Page 64,** © Michael Newman/PhotoEdit; **Page 65,** © Tom & Dee Ann McCarthy/Corbis; **Page 66,** RubberBall Productions.